HEINEMANN School Management

CW00968958

The Head of Department's Handbook

JEFF JONES
SUE KIRKHAM
MAZDA JENKIN

The Head of Department's Handbook

Heinemann Educational
Halley Court, Jordan Hill, Oxford OX2 8EJ
a division of Reed Educational & Professional Publishing Ltd

OXFORD MELBOURNE AUCKLAND
JOHANNESBURG BLANTYRE GABORONE
IBADAN PORTSMOUTH (NH) USA CHICAGO

First published 1996

00 99
10 9 8 7 6 5

A catalogue record for this book is available from the British Library

ISBN 0 435 80050 7

The authors

Mazda Jenkin is Headteacher of Rising Brook High School, Stone, Staffordshire.

Sue Kirkham is Headteacher of the Woodrush High School, Hereford and Worcester.

Jeff Jones is Principal Lecturer at the University of Wolverhampton and formerly an Inspector for Hereford and Worcester.

Typeset by TechType
Printed by Athenæum Press Ltd, Gateshead

Contents

Introduction

The purpose of this Head of Department's handbook is to provide guidance to you, as a Head of Department, in the firm belief that the quality of pupil learning depends critically on your leadership.

The middle management role of Heads of Department is increasingly being seen as crucial to the success of secondary schools. While traditionally Heads of Department have concentrated on the management of their subject area, they have become more aware of the need to develop a range of allied management skills. This awareness has been heightened with the introduction of local management, the National Curriculum, appraisal and OFSTED inspection, as well as moves to make schools more accountable and competitive.

In many ways the role is a daunting one. Potentially, it is also a highly rewarding one. Although administration can occupy a substantial amount of your time, you are still in direct and constant contact with pupils. It is true that you are held responsible for much of what goes on in your subject area, but equally you are in the enviable position of sharing the excitement and achievement of pupils and staff firsthand.

This handbook has been compiled to assist you with the many and varied aspects of your role. It contains guidance, suggestions and examples of good practice. It is intended as a practical resource, which should enable you to keep your administration under control and to focus on the critical aspects of the leadership of a department. There are samples of proformas for your use at the end of the book in the Resource Bank.

The authors would like to thank all of those colleagues who have been prepared to share their experiences and practices.

1 The role of the Head of Department

Introduction

'A leader shapes and shares a vision which gives point to the work of others.' (Charles Handy, 1989)

The primary role of managers at all levels is to lead, and the primary task of leadership is to provide vision, to achieve a commitment to a set of values, and to guide and inspire colleagues.

But, as a leader, it is equally important to remember that your vision must be brought to reality.

The Head of Department's role now, more than ever, is complex and demanding. In addition to being a sound administrator, a Head of Department will need to display a range of organisational and interpersonal skills if the department is to be managed successfully.

As Head of Department, you are likely to have a description of your role and its associated responsibilities, like the example on the next page. However, the effectiveness with which the role is performed is likely to be judged by your ability to:

- analyse the current curriculum provision, taking account of statutory requirements, staffing, organisation, and the needs of the school as a whole
- decide what improvements and developments are needed, together with the implications for staffing and resources

- order priorities and set long-term targets with interim objectives clearly stated
- monitor and evaluate the quality of teaching and learning within the department
- anticipate and clearly communicate ideas in a way which will secure the commitment of others.

Job description

SAMPLE JOB DESCRIPTION

POST: Head of Department

Principal Responsibilities:

1. **To plan, implement and review the curriculum within the framework of the National Curriculum and the school's policies.**
2. **To oversee the teaching within the department through the preparation of schemes of work and monitoring performance of students during lessons.**
3. **To contribute to teaching within the department.**
4. **To ensure that students' work is regularly assessed and their achievements recorded.**
5. **To control and direct the ordering, storage and use of materials, equipment, books, etc. and to account for spending within the budget to the Deputy Head in charge of finance.**
6. **To oversee the work of teaching and non-teaching staff assigned to the department and to advise and assist the Headteacher in matters of staff appointments and appraisal.**
7. **To oversee the professional development of departmental staff through a process of guidance, delegation and consultation. To take part in appraisal arrangements and in the review process leading to the preparation of the school's Development Plan.**

8. To support members of the department who may be having problems with individual students or classes; to ensure student discipline is maintained in order to establish lessons so that meaningful learning can take place.
9. As a senior member of staff, to take a full part in the formulation and implementation of school policy and in the whole life of the school.
10. To attend meetings of the Heads of Department Committee in accordance with the school's time budget.
11. To chair regular department team meetings as directed within the school's time budget and ensure that minutes are taken with copies being given to the Headteacher.
12. To liaise closely with the Deputy Head in charge of timetables with regard to the allocation of curriculum time to the department, and also with regard to the assignment of appropriate staff to courses.
13. To liaise with the school's Examinations Officer and Deputy Head in charge of examinations over entries for GCSE, GCE Advanced Level and other examinations, and National Curriculum tests at Key Stage 3.
14. To implement the school's Information Technology Policy.
15. To implement school policies for Learning Support including the needs of the most and the least able.
16. To ensure that the department's teaching area presents a stimulating environment.
17. To supervise the use and care of all teaching spaces assigned to the department including the adherence to relevant health and safety regulations.
18. To supervise the work of, and give professional guidance to, any student or NQT assigned to the department, supplying written reports to the appropriate Deputy Head upon request.
19. To oversee liaison:
    (i) within school
    (ii) with contributory schools and with other middle and high schools
    (iii) with parents
    (iv) with other institutions such as colleges of further education, local industry, etc.
20. To ensure that there are equal opportunities for all.

Evaluating your performance

As a new Head of Department you are likely to possess many of the necessary skills and qualities to meet the challenge of running an effective department. To ensure an effective department, it is possible to develop others through class observation, increased experience, and in-service training.

A useful starting point is to consider your own development needs by evaluating your current performance using the questionnaire below. It

Self evaluation questionnaire RB1

Rate your performance using the scale:
1 = very good 2 = good 3 = satisfactory 4 = some weakness 5 = area for improvement

Be honest with yourself – and don't underestimate your abilities!

1 Ability to communicate with members of the department team	1 ☐	2 ☐	3 ☐	4 ☐	5 ☐
2 Ability to communicate ideas in writing	1 ☐	2 ☐	3 ☐	4 ☐	5 ☐
3 Ability to communicate ideas orally	1 ☐	2 ☐	3 ☐	4 ☐	5 ☐
4 Ability to represent the views of the department team to the Senior Management	1 ☐	2 ☐	3 ☐	4 ☐	5 ☐
5 Ability to represent the views of the Senior Management Team to the department	1 ☐	2 ☐	3 ☐	4 ☐	5 ☐
6 Ability to organise the administrative work of the department	1 ☐	2 ☐	3 ☐	4 ☐	5 ☐
7 Ability to delegate responsibilities to others in the department team	1 ☐	2 ☐	3 ☐	4 ☐	5 ☐
8 Ability to chair departmental meetings	1 ☐	2 ☐	3 ☐	4 ☐	5 ☐
9 Ability to handle difficult members of the department	1 ☐	2 ☐	3 ☐	4 ☐	5 ☐
10 Ability to provide constructive criticism	1 ☐	2 ☐	3 ☐	4 ☐	5 ☐
11 Ability to accept constructive criticism	1 ☐	2 ☐	3 ☐	4 ☐	5 ☐
12 Ability to listen to others	1 ☐	2 ☐	3 ☐	4 ☐	5 ☐
13 Ability to persuade others to your point of view	1 ☐	2 ☐	3 ☐	4 ☐	5 ☐
14 Ability to plan ahead, setting realistic targets for departmental improvement	1 ☐	2 ☐	3 ☐	4 ☐	5 ☐
15 Ability to implement agreed plans	1 ☐	2 ☐	3 ☐	4 ☐	5 ☐
16 Ability to solve problems	1 ☐	2 ☐	3 ☐	4 ☐	5 ☐
17 Ability to use time effectively	1 ☐	2 ☐	3 ☐	4 ☐	5 ☐
18 Ability to manage stress	1 ☐	2 ☐	3 ☐	4 ☐	5 ☐
19 Ability to identify problems	1 ☐	2 ☐	3 ☐	4 ☐	5 ☐
20 Ability to understand whole school issues	1 ☐	2 ☐	3 ☐	4 ☐	5 ☐

could form the basis of your personal development plan which you should discuss with your school's Professional Development Co-ordinator. There is a photocopiable version of the questionnaire in the Resource Bank at the back of this book.

Extract from a Head of Department's personal development plan

PERSONAL DEVELOPMENT PLAN		
Area for development	**Targets**	**INSET required**
Chairing meetings	■ **circulate agenda before meeting** ■ **make sure everyone has a say** ■ **summarise agreements** ■ **keep meeting to time**	**Course or opportunity to observe chairing of other meetings in school**

Whether or not you use this approach, it is important to keep your own development needs under review. You will want to keep up to date with your subject and attend subject association and exam board meetings. You will also want to develop your skills as a manager and administrator.

Your school's Professional Development Co-ordinator will have details of courses available locally and nationally and you might like to consider a course with a higher qualification. Many higher educational establishments now offer modular Master's Degree courses which may enable you to work in your own time and spread the cost of the qualification. Alternatively, you might like to explore the development opportunities in your own school. Can you gain confidence and management expertise by working with other staff on whole-school initiatives, e.g. a working party to develop new approaches to managing student behaviour?

It is the role of middle management staff to provide leadership, maintain morale, encourage staff development and facilitate co-operation between staff. Establishing good working relationships is the key to building an efficient and effective team.

2 Evaluation and planning

Introduction

All schools now produce some form of School Development Plan. Evaluating the performance of the department and planning for development in the context of whole-school priorities are essential responsibilities for the Head of Department.

The Head of Department needs to develop:

- a clear overview of the successes/failures within the department
- an understanding of whole-school priorities and issues which affect, and interrelate with, the department's plans and performance.

Auditing the department's performance

The first stage of this evaluation and planning process is a systematic audit of the work of the department in the preceding year. This forms part of a development cycle which can operate throughout the year. The whole cycle will help to:

- identify the reasons for successes and failures
- develop plans for the next year(s)
- set targets to gauge the success of the plans.

An example of a development cycle

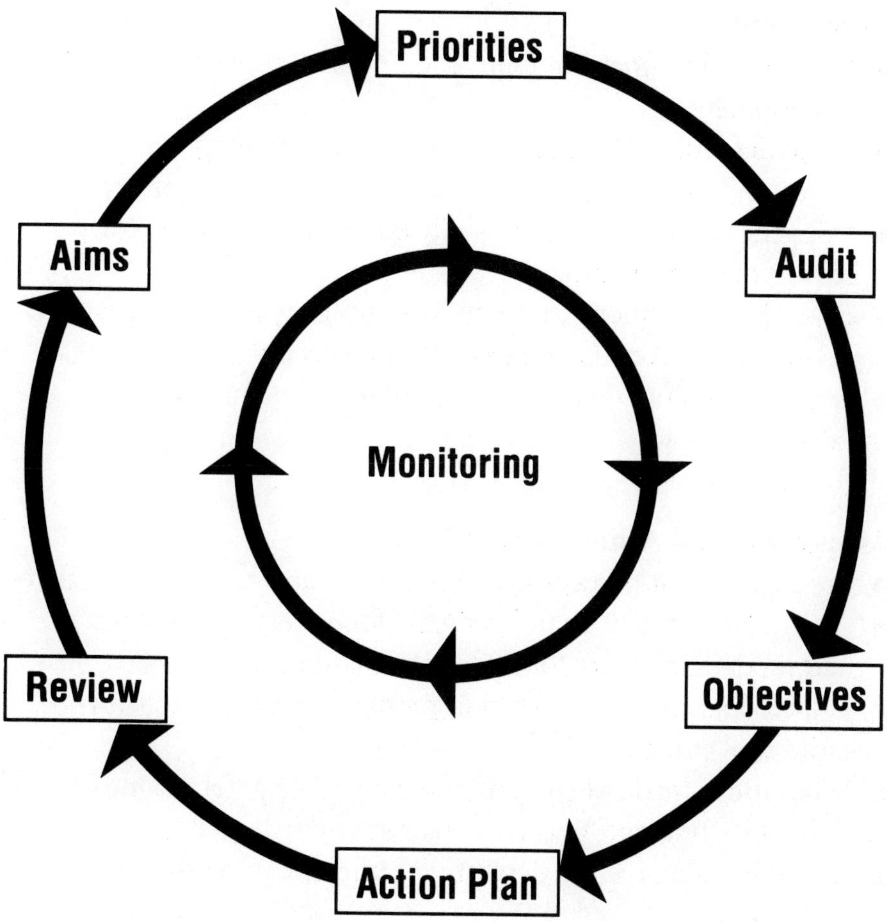

Auditing the work of the department can be done in writing, but it is important to make time to talk to staff individually and collectively about achievements and difficulties in the previous year.

The department's performance can be audited using an audit document like the one which follows. The document can be filled in for senior managers and discussed with them in a process of evaluation before the development plan is written. Alternatively, it can be used by a Head of Department with members of the departmental team in preparation for a team meeting to review progress. Wherever possible, evidence should be sought to support the responses to the questions.

ANNUAL DEPARTMENTAL AUDIT

Curriculum

- Does the department monitor the progress of planned development?
- Is the department meeting the curriculum development targets in last year's plan? (Indicate successes/problem areas)
- Does the department successfully contribute to the delivery of Information Technology?
- Does the department successfully contribute to the delivery of other cross-curricular areas? (Please specify)
- Is the curriculum delivered appropriate to the needs of:
  (a) the less able
  (b) the more able?

Assessment and Achievement

- Are department procedures for assessing and recording effective?
- Are the department's arrangements for collecting evidence and moderating work for KS3 assessments effective?
- Is the department successful in monitoring the progress of individual students?
- What use is made of student assessment? (e.g. for diagnosing difficulties or identifying particular strengths)
- Are all members of the department implementing the agreed marking policy?
- Are procedures for identifying and rewarding achievement at all levels of ability effective?
- Are the criteria for achievement clear to students?
- Does the department ensure that information about student achievement is passed on to:
  (a) parents
  (b) pastoral staff?

Resources

- Does the department monitor the use of resources effectively?
- Does resource allocation within the department support agreed targets for development?

- Is there an appropriate balance within the department of spending on maintenance and spending on development?
- Is the accommodation allocated to the department adequate for its needs?
- Are classrooms and teachers' areas organised to facilitate teaching and learning, i.e. tidy, clear of unused or unnecessary furniture and fittings, properly equipped and maintained, etc.?

Staffing and Staff Development

- Is there a good match of staff expertise and teaching groups? (Indicate successes and problem areas)
- Has the department received INSET as requested in the departmental plan?
- Was the INSET received useful? Has it helped/changed practice? Was the result of any INSET disseminated within the department?

Public Exams

- Does the performance of students taught by members of the department match
  (a) predicted grades
  (b) performance of the same students in other subjects?
- Do the exam syllabuses allow the students the best available opportunities to demonstrate what they can achieve?

Organisation

- Is the way in which teaching and learning are organised within the department satisfactory? Are there any problems?

Liaison

- Are the department's liaison arrangements with feeder schools effective in ensuring continuity and progression?
- Do feeder schools have copies of the department's scheme of work?

Communication

- Is formal/informal communication within the department and with others effective, e.g.:
  (a) parents
  (b) governors
  (c) senior managers
  (d) others?

The audit can form the basis of the department's evaluation of its progress and achievement during the year. Discussing the reasons for successes and failures can help the department team to begin planning its next moves and the best ways to achieve its targets.

Identifying priorities

The process of auditing the performance of the department will lead on to identifying the department's priorities for further development. You will need to ask yourself and the department team:

- What will be the main areas for development within the department in the:
  - next year?
  - next 2–4 years?
- What is the main purpose of change?
- How will developments be monitored and evaluated?

In your role as Head of Department you will also need to consider whole-school priorities. These may be generated:

- by the external context in which the school operates, e.g. changes to the National Curriculum, changes to the syllabuses from examination boards, alterations to appraisal regulations
- by the school's senior managers based on the whole-school audit, e.g. liaison with feeder schools, curriculum continuity and progression. In this case the Head of Department will be expected to include these proposals in the departmental development plan.

In practice, the Head of Department often faces competing and multiple priorities and it can be difficult to decide what to place as the highest priority. The values of the Head of Department are important here since decisions are usually affected by personal and professional values and preferences, e.g.:

- if the Head of Department is very student-centred in approach, priorities which are of immediate benefit to students may be given the highest ranking
- if the Head of Department is very committed to democracy, the decision may be made according to the views of the majority in the team.

However the decision is made, it is important to discuss the issues involved with the department team and to clarify the values behind the decision to avoid misunderstandings.

Values are a set of principles and standards belonging to an individual or group.

If you are uncertain about the values which shape your decision making, think about decisions you have made about the department and try to identify the reasons why these decisions are important to you.

THE CONNECTION BETWEEN VALUES AND DECISIONS

Decision	Reason
Students' work to be displayed in all classrooms.	Belief in emphasising the value or worth of students' work.
Courses to have a detailed scheme of work.	Belief in importance of communicating what we are teaching/desire to make learning experience for students explicit.
All staff in the department to use the same marking scheme.	Coherence more important than individual teacher freedom in this respect.

ACTIVITY

List 5 decisions you have made about the department recently and try to identify why they were important to you.

Decision	Reason
1.	
2.	
3.	
4.	
5.	

Writing the department's development plan

Once priorities for the following year have been identified, it is possible to write the formal departmental development plan. Formats for these vary from school to school. Two examples follow on pages 13 and 14.

Whatever the format, the Head of Department will have to:

- express a commitment to action in the form of targets
- identify the resource implications of the targets proposed
- identify success criteria.

Targets needs to be **SMART**:

Specific
Measurable
Achievable
Realistic
Timelined.

Departmental development plan 199 /9

RB2

Organisation (broad outline)	Staff co-ordinator INSET implications Resource and financial implications Success criteria
Curriculum (target areas for development and planned stages of implementation)	Staff co-ordinator INSET implications Resource and financial implications Success criteria
Assessment	Staff co-ordinator INSET implications Resource and financial implications Success criteria
Whole-school priorities	Staff co-ordinator INSET implications Resource and financial implications Success criteria

There is a photocopiable version of this planner in the Resource Bank at the end of this book.

Extracts from a sample development plan

Departmental development plan **RB3**

Priority	Improve student success at 'A' level by changing exam syllabus
Targets	1. Contact exam boards for up-to-date syllabuses by the end of term 2. Speak to LEA adviser about 'A' level courses by the end of term 3. Visit a school offering a modular syllabus early next term 4. Arrange department meeting to decide which course to adopt w/c Jan 30th
Resource implications (including INSET)	Cost of syllabuses Cost of supply cover and travel Additional resources to run new course = £200 INSET on 'A' level course = £150
Monitoring	Review course at departmental meetings Check student progress via interim and end of year reports
Success criteria	New 'A' level course adopted following thorough research Increased student success at 'A' level (longer term)

There is a blank photocopiable version of this planner in the Resource Bank at the end of this book.

Monitoring progress

Heads of Department should constantly monitor standards of teaching and learning. This may include any of the following:

- lesson observation
- checking of staff record books
- checking of staff homework records
- checking by collecting pupils' exercise books/files
- standardisation of the assessment of pupils' work.

These exercises will enable you to ascertain that departmental policies and schemes of work are being followed.

The process will be more effective if:

- you can discuss your findings with an 'outsider', (some senior staff, or you could use an Inspector/Advisor/Consultant)
- your findings are regularly discussed at departmental meetings.

New priorities (as identified in your development plan) will need particularly careful monitoring, so that you can take action to keep these on course. Consider the example below.

WAYS OF MONITORING DEVELOPMENT PRIORITIES

Priority	Monitoring
Improve student success at A level by changing exam syllabus.	1 Check student performance regularly and compare with previous years.
	2 Make a survey of students' views.
	3 Use departmental discussion at regular meetings.
	4 Seek outside observation e.g. school senior manager or subject inspector.

Regular and systematic evaluation will support you in managing your department effectively.

3 Managing staff

Introduction

In your capacity as Head of Department, you have a very important role to play in the management and development of your staff. The way in which department members work together as a team and function effectively as individuals will depend to a great extent on your ability to motivate and inspire them.

Important factors in staff management include:

- an understanding of your own strengths and weaknesses
- an understanding of the strengths of team members
- the recruitment, selection and induction of new staff
- developing staff skills and expertise
- delegating responsibilities
- deploying staff appropriately

Staff audit

You will need to know the qualifications, job descriptions, recent INSET experience and strengths of the members of your Department – teaching and non-teaching staff. To help you with this task, you will find it helpful to:

- obtain details from central files (if possible)
- keep records of how you deploy your staff each year and the reasons for the allocation of groups
- update information regularly through staff development interviews.

Staff record sheet RB4

Date ______________ Name ______________

Year ______________ Department ______________

Qualifications

Year appointed

Classes taught

Contact ratio

Exam syllabuses/ courses taught

Extra responsibilities

Extra curriculum activities

Appraisal process

INSET/courses attended

Other information

There is a photocopiable version of this record sheet in the Resource Bank at the end of this book.

Staff development interviews

These will help you to:

- build a positive relationship with individuals
- keep accurate records
- explore with individuals their concept of their own role, their strengths and weaknesses
- understand the individual's motivation and ambitions
- emphasise the importance you attach to staff development
- remain up to date with the outcome of the individual's last appraisal interview.

The interview:

- should be conducted in comfortable surroundings where you are unlikely to be disturbed
- should have sufficient allocated time
- should be conducted with reference to records (job description, INSET etc.)
- should have you listening rather than talking for the majority of the time.

You will find it useful to use a proforma to collect information during the interview. There is a photocopiable version of the plan opposite in the Resource Bank at the end of this book.

Personal staff development plan (RB5)

Name ______________________ Date ____________

Past year (courses, INSET, committees, curriculum development initiatives, departmental responsibilities, etc.)

Teaching/Tutorial commitment this year (age, subject, levels, exam courses, etc.)

Interest/Experience in other subject areas or other levels

Future career development

Personal INSET/ development needs

Whole School/ Development needs

Action Plan

Signed ______________________ (Head of Department)

Signed ______________________ (Staff)

Identifying priorities

Once you have completed an audit of current staff, you will be in a position to decide on priorities for staff development. You will also be in a position to decide on the need for new staff. Before doing either, however, there are some points to consider:

- The Headteacher may have different perceptions of the roles and responsibilities of individual members of staff.
- There may be whole-school planning issues connected with future staffing needs, pupil numbers, etc.
- The Professional Development Coordinator will have information about courses, funding, local and national initiatives and previous INSET.
- The school bursar/financial administrator will have information about the way courses are funded and money available.

Planning

Once you have agreed your priorities with senior managers you need to begin more detailed planning for their implementation. These are some of the issues which will arise:

Recruitment, selection, induction and retention

Recruitment and selection

Heads of Department should influence the recruitment and selection of new members of staff by:

- identifying the needs of the department
- supplying the headteacher with accurate information for advertisements and job descriptions
- ensuring that candidates have opportunities to visit the department and meet other department members.

If you are involved in shortlisting and interviewing, consider the following:

- existing departmental strengths and weaknesses
- curricular needs
- team 'fit' and candidates' values
- expertise offered/future potential
- other contributions, curricular and extra-curricular.

Induction

Induction of new staff should be considered a high priority for a Head of Department.

New members of the department will settle more quickly and become more effective members of the team when you:

- ensure that they are supplied with departmental handbooks, policies and schemes of work in advance
- allocate departmental mentors for each new teacher, student, supply teacher (NB You do not necessarily have to be the mentor,

especially in a large department. A good teacher with several years' experience can be very helpful to a NQT).

The crucial thing from your perspective is that you:

- have an overview of the progress made by a new teacher and whether there are any problems
- use the expertise of staff who, while being new to the school, will have particular strengths and different experiences to offer.

Retention

You should use your knowledge, skills and expertise to motivate and retain those members of the department whose work you value. This may include:

- being aware of whole-school staff policies
- taking appropriate action to ensure they gain points available
- delegating real responsibilities
- recommending appropriate professional development.

Staff will feel more motivated if they:

- understand why and how decisions have been made (for example, in the allocation of classes)
- are consulted during the decision-making period
- feel that the outcomes are fair.

Delegation of responsibilities

As a new Head of Department it sometimes seems that you are responsible for doing everything in the department. However, it is important both for the effective management of the department and for the career development of individual staff to delegate appropriately.

The Head of Department's role is to co-ordinate and support staff in developing areas of expertise. Task rotation should also be considered.

The following are examples of responsibilities which can be delegated:

- information technology
- equal opportunities
- stock control/ordering
- set lists
- specific courses/years or key stages

- liaison with feeder schools
- learning support/special needs
- exam entries
- exam moderation
- exam preparation (internal)
- investigation and development of new courses
- development of industrial links
- appraisal co-ordination
- flexible learning
- equipment
- classroom/corridor display
- INSET co-ordination
- management of teaching materials and resources
- non-teaching staff welfare

A discussion of areas of responsibility should form part of the annual staff-development interview. It may be necessary to negotiate with individual staff to establish responsibilities which both parties find acceptable. Successful negotiation depends on:

- being able to separate the individual from the issue
- clear identification of issues and priorities
- selecting solutions on their merit
- resisting pressure and avoiding provocation
- demonstrating empathy and focused listening
- effective summarising
- demonstrating mutual respect and trust

The negotiation of areas of responsibility should result in the implementation of the negotiated agreement, and the list of delegated responsibilities should be published in the departmental handbook.

INSET

INSET is a means of presenting staff with opportunities for developing their knowledge, skills and attitudes.

In planning INSET you should:

- include a summary of the requests for INSET in the department's development plan. These requests should be fully costed (course fees, travel expenses, supply cover, reading and INSET materials).
- encourage members of staff to keep their own personal development plan, which can then be discussed and up-dated each year.
- seek advice from your PDC and other relevant subject specialists and plan carefully for INSET days in school for your department. The form RB6 (which follows on page 24) will help you to provide all the necessary information to senior managers. There is a photocopiable version of this form in the Resource Bank at the end of this book.
- evaluate the effectiveness of the training and ensure that steps are taken to ensure appropriate evaluation of the outcome. This can be achieved either through reports at Departmental meetings, or the use of an evaluation form such as RB7 (which follows on page 25).

Departmental INSET planning form RB6

Departmental INSET ______________________________ 199__

Department ______________________________

Topic

Aims of the day

Programme:
(with details of timing for morning and afternoon sessions)

Provider in-house/visitor

Cost

Location/venue
(rooms and facilities required)

Signed ______________________________

There is a photocopiable version of this form in the Resource Bank at the end of this book.

INSET course evaluation form **RB7**

Name ______________________________

Title of course ______________________________

Course providers ______________________________

Date ______________ Venue ______________

Funding for course:

Course aims:

How far did the course meet its aims and your INSET needs?

What action(s) if any are you going to take as a result of attending this course?

Would you recommend this course to other staff?

There is a photocopiable version of this form in the Resource Bank at the end of this book.

Writing the department's staff development policy

The department's staff development policy should express the department's commitment to the importance of in-service training and other forms of staff development. It needs to be consistent with the whole-school policy on staff development and should include the following areas:

1 The identification of the training needs of the department in relation to:

- National Curriculum
- assessment
- new courses or syllabuses
- differentiation
- special needs
- information technology
- relevant cross-curricular issues
- health and safety
- whole-school priorities expressed in the school's development plan.

2 The identification of the individual needs of members of staff determined through staff development interviews and appraisal. There should be a mechanism for prioritising and combining departmental and individual needs bearing in mind that the primary aim of all staff development should be the enhancement of the quality of education provided.

3 The planning of in-service training based on the priorities identified. In-service training might include:

- national courses/conferences
- LEA/HE courses
- distance learning courses
- membership of subject associations and the purchase of subject journals
- the purchase of training materials/books
- membership of collaborative working parties

- use of departmental meeting time
- visiting speakers/trainers
- visits to other schools to investigate good practice
- sharing of good practice within the department
- sharing of expertise available within the school, e.g. I.T. Co-ordinator, Special Needs Co-ordinator
- development projects
- 'shadowing' a more senior member of staff.

Provision should be made for evaluation and assessment of the impact of the training on the quality of teaching and learning within the department.

4 Departmental arrangements for the induction and monitoring of students, newly qualified staff, new staff and supply or temporary teachers.

5 Arrangements for training and development of non-teaching staff, where relevant.

ACTIVITY

Look at the following whole-school staff development policy or your own school's staff development policy. Consider the points raised in this section, and then draft your department's staff development plan, making it consistent with the whole-school approach.

SAMPLE WHOLE-SCHOOL STAFF DEVELOPMENT POLICY

AIMS

To provide continuing development of the professional knowledge, skills and commitment of staff in order to improve the education of the pupils.

To clarify the staff's involvement in and awareness of:

i) the school's philosophy, aims and objectives, and
ii) the school development plan.

To encourage individual teachers to plan their careers and to identify and exploit career opportunities.

RESPONSIBILITY FOR STAFF DEVELOPMENT

1. Professional Leadership

It is part of the job description of the Headteacher and all staff with responsibility for colleagues that they help to develop the professional knowledge, skills and aspirations of individual staff within their area of responsibility.

2. Staff Development Committee (SDC)

This committee provides a forum for discussion of staff needs. It attempts to ascertain the needs and to co-ordinate and plan group and whole-school INSET activities. The SDC is comprised of the professional development co-ordinator (PCD), one representative from the pastoral group, one representative from the policy group and five other staff. Staff members to be elected biennially. Staff may be co-opted if a committee member leaves between elections.

The function of the SDC is specifically to advise the Headteacher on:

- staff training, including secondment, industrial placement, short courses and internal staff development
- institutional needs
- teacher education/occasional days.

Apart from formally organised staff development interviews, the Headteacher and senior staff are always willing to provide support and counselling on an individual and confidential basis if required.

WHOLE-SCHOOL IN-SERVICE TRAINING

1. Teacher Education Days

These take place regularly. They provide an opportunity for a range of activities including visiting speakers, discussion groups, workshops, and plenary sessions based on themes decided in consultation with the staff, and in support of the school development plan.

2. Staff Meetings, Consultation Groups and Briefings

Staff meetings take place, as needed, before consultation group meetings. They provide a forum for dissemination of information and consultation over day-to-day matters. In small consultation groups, staff consider issues of relevance to the school plan and/or school planning. A short written report from each group is given to the senior management team. Directed time allocated to staff consultation groups may also be used for departments or pastoral teams to consider whole-school issues. Briefings take place at break every Monday in the staffroom. The Headteacher informs staff of any matters of immediate relevance and offers advice where necessary. Colleagues also publicise specific needs or concerns at these sessions. A written record of the briefing is put on the staff noticeboard. The deputies and senior teachers undertake break duty on Mondays.

IN-SERVICE TRAINING FOR FUNCTIONAL GROUPS

1. Departments

Heads of Department encourage the development of their teams' teaching and academic skills by a variety of means. These include co-operation in planning courses, encouraging attendance at INSET courses, arranging visits to other schools and developing mutual lesson observation and analysis. They also keep their members informed of policy discussion in the policy group meetings. In addition, Heads of Departments organise and are involved in:

i) regular departmental meetings
ii) departmental INSET meetings
iii) pyramid liaison meetings

In particular they will have specific responsibility for newly qualified teachers (NQTs) in their subject areas and will be closely involved in the compilation of any NQT report. Heads of Department will be actively concerned with the integration of any new staff within their departments.

2. Year Groups

Heads of Year encourage the development of their team's pastoral skills and organise and get involved in:

i) regular tutor meetings
ii) occasional school-focused courses as needs are identified.

They also keep their tutor team informed of the discussions of the pastoral group.

3. NQTs and Staff New To the School

The PDC organises an induction programme, which includes a regular series of meetings throughout the first half-term to introduce staff to the organisational structure of the school and to provide a forum for discussion of challenges arising in the first year of teaching. The further induction of experienced staff is dealt with according to their needs.

4. The School Development Plan

All members of staff are involved in the drawing up of the school development plan. Department/Pastoral targets clearly state INSET implications. At regular intervals, discussions take place between staff and the senior management team so that targets can be reviewed.

SCHOOL-BASED COURSES

INSET takes place in school on a voluntary basis when a need is identified. Any member of staff may suggest a course to the SDC.

INDIVIDUAL OPPORTUNITIES

Details of any INSET courses are available on the staff noticeboard or in publications (such as the TES) available in the library. They include degree courses, shorter courses organised by LEAs, consultants, the DFEE and part-time or evening courses at universities or teachers' centres. Before applying for any course, whether during or out of school time, staff should consult the PDC who will advise about the necessary steps to be taken. Any staff who are interested in applying for secondment or an industrial placement should first discuss their interest with the Headteacher.

STAFF APPRAISAL

All permanent staff with three responsibility points or more should have received appraisal training. Appraisal takes place on a line management basis. The Headteacher regularly summarises INSET requirements and liaises with the PDC. Full details are laid out in the schools' appraisal policy statement.

STANDING COMMITTEES

There are three standing committees:

i) the policy group (Headteacher, deputies, SEN co-ordinator and heads of major departments)
ii) the pastoral group (Headteacher, deputies, SEN co-ordinator and heads of year)
iii) the staff development committee (the PDC, one head of department, one head of year and five other elected members of staff).

The Heads holds regular pyramid meetings with the Headteachers of pyramid first and middle schools. In addition, the curriculum deputy and curriculum representatives from the feeder middle schools, meet twice a term.

Appraisal

All schools are required to be involved in statutory appraisal. As Head of Department you will be appraised and you may be responsible for appraising staff within your area. The appraisal process for all teachers is shown below.

THE APPRAISAL PROCESS FOR TEACHERS

Initial meetings between Appraiser(s) and Appraisee

↓

Appraisee self-appraisal
Classroom/task observation(s)
Collection of other data

↓

Appraisal interview
Target setting
Appraisal statement produced

↓

Follow-up discussion between Appraiser(s) and Appraisee
Professional development activities

↓

Formal review meeting
Additions to appraisal statement
Follow-up support and professional development

Schools will have their own programmes of staff training for appraisal but the skills of classroom observation are ones which a Head of Department should develop. They can be employed in the wider context of supporting and developing staff.

Classroom observation

Before any observation, you should be aware of the:

- nature of the class (size, groupings, special needs, specific problems)
- the way in which the session to be observed fits into the overall curriculum plan

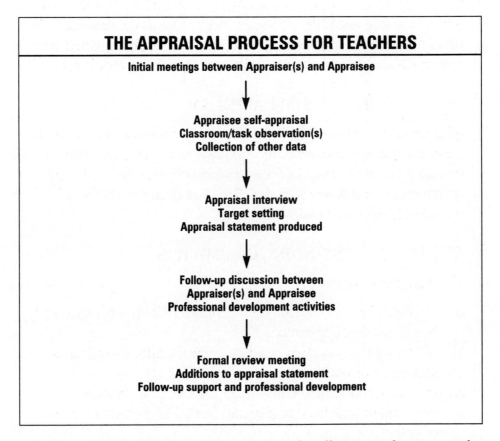

- teaching focus for the session being observed
- resources available and constraints
- tasks to be undertaken by the pupils.

You should have agreed with your colleague:

- the duration and purpose of the observation
- specific areas to be focused on
- the form of observation (participatory or non-participatory)
- the way in which the observation is recorded
- the time for feedback and further planning
- realistic objectives.

During the observation session you should:

- make notes, perhaps in a duplicate book, so that your colleague can have a copy
- ensure that you can see all the pupils
- sit outside the teacher's direct line of vision
- strictly adhere to the agreed objectives and focus
- avoid active participation unless this has been agreed
- remain for the whole of the session.

Following the observation session you should:

- make brief oral comments at the end of the session
- make arrangements to give formal, constructive feedback
- make time for careful reflection and evaluation before meeting with your colleague
- focus the feedback on the action, rather than the person
- focus the feedback on concrete observations rather than on inferences and assumptions
- resist the temptation to make value judgements
- direct the feedback at aspects of behaviour or performance about which your colleague can do something
- consider whether the objectives were realised
- gauge whether the arrangements were effective and allowed detailed observation
- decide whether sufficient evidence was collected to make informal judgements and whether any further information is required.

Your colleague should:

- think about the nature of the observation and its objectives
- consider whether it affected the pupil behaviour/performance
- decide whether it affected teacher style and effectiveness
- reflect on the aspects of the lesson which were successful and those which s/he would like to improve.

As a Head of Department your aim must be to ensure high standards of teaching and learning. This can only be done by working with or through your staff. Therefore, effective staff management must be a high priority for you.

4 Managing resources for teaching and learning

Introduction

Managing resources so that they support the teaching and learning within the department is an important task for all Heads of Department. Chapter 3 covers the management of the most important resource: your staff. This chapter covers the management of the department's other resources and considers the following aspects:

- auditing and evaluating existing resources
- securing adequate finance, time, accommodation and staffing to enable the department to run effectively
- ordering and taking care of teaching/learning materials
- ensuring that staff and pupils have access to appropriate materials for the courses offered and the pupils' levels of ability
- looking after equipment and ensuring that health and safety procedures are followed.

Resource management is often seen as a cycle, as shown in the diagram on page 36. However you need to be aware that the resource cycle is based on the financial year and not the academic year. This means that as Head of Department, you will need to start thinking about the courses you wish to run next year at the beginning of the current academic year so that you can secure the appropriate resources.

Resource Management Cycle

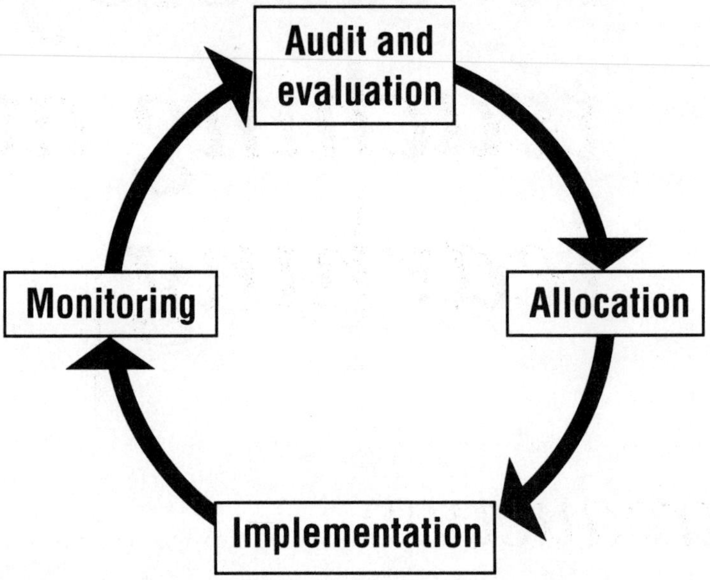

Auditing resources

The first stage of any resource management cycle is for the Head of Department to conduct an audit of existing resources.

Stocktaking

This audit should include the annual stocktaking of textbooks and other resources for teaching and learning. It is helpful to analyse existing stocks of materials in terms of their suitability for different groups and years using a stock list like the example below.

Stock list for books **RB8**

No	Title	Author	Ability/level

There is a photocopiable version of this stock list in the Resource Bank at the end of this book.

Stock lists help to show where there are gaps in the department's provision as well as enabling you to analyse the scale of any losses from the previous year. The stock list should be updated every year.

Accommodation

The rooms which the department uses are part of its overall resources. Their state of repair, the appropriateness of furniture and the standard of classroom display should be included in your audit. The care of departmental accommodation also says much about your standards and effectiveness in maintaining a good learning environment for pupils. Not all rooms are purpose built and equipped with the latest technology, but most can be kept clean, uncluttered and provide stimulating displays of pupils' work and learning materials. Graffiti and broken furniture need to be removed immediately before the situation worsens and staff need to be encouraged to take pride in, and responsibility for, their teaching areas.

ACTIVITY

Checklist for auditing use of accommodation	**Yes/No**
Do all members of the department have appropriate teaching rooms?	
Are teaching rooms allocated to staff on a rational and fair basis?	
Do all departmental rooms have displays of pupils' work?	
Are rooms clean and tidy and free from graffiti?	
Do all departmental rooms have appropriate furniture?	
Do all members of the department have keys to storerooms and classrooms?	

Securing resources

The next stage of the resource management cycle is to secure adequate resources for the work of the department. Resources are available from a variety of external sources including European and national initiatives, the LEA and in some cases, directly from the government. However, for most Heads of Department, resources are dependent on the school's budget for teaching and learning.

Making a capitation bid

In many schools the Head of Department has to secure a share of the school's teaching/learning budget by making a bid for what is often called 'capitation'. The term implies that funds are allocated on a 'per capita' basis i.e. on the numbers taught. In fact the criteria for awarding funds can vary widely and can include the Headteacher's subjective judgement, past practice, legal requirements, the number of pupils or teaching periods taught, whole-school priorities, micro-political considerations, or the concerns expressed by governors or parents.

Bids are made in various formats. In some schools, Heads of Department have to cost departmental activities, e.g. field trips, the use of supply teachers to cover for orals, or the cost of exam entries, and include these in their bid. Bids are often unsuccessful if they:

- ignore the procedure and format used in the school
- fail to give adequate details
- do not take account of the criteria being used to allocate funding.

You will need to know the criteria on which resources are allocated in your school. You can then adopt an appropriate strategy for making a successful bid for the department. If a rational system is used in the school, resources may be allocated:

- on an incremental basis, i.e. a percentage increase on the previous year's funding
- on a 'zero base' approach where no on-going or regular costs are taken for granted. Instead, the department has to justify all aspects of its proposed spending

- according to a formula such as pupil periods taught, possibly taking into account practical subjects needing expensive resources
- using a 'programme' approach where resources are allocated to meet the requirements of an agreed list of priorities or programmes (usually published in the department's development plan)
- using a mixture of approaches.

POSSIBLE STRATEGIES FOR SECURING DEPARTMENTAL RESOURCES

Criteria for resource allocation	Departmental strategy
Incremental	Request an additional percentage increase related to e.g. any percentage increase in inflation or to any percentage increase in the overall budget.
Zero base	Ensure that all aspects of the department's work are costed and included in the request for resources.
Formula	Calculate the number of pupil periods taught in the department, making a case for a special weighting if the department uses a lot of expensive materials.
Programme	Ensure that the departmental development plan and the request for resources are clearly linked.

Bids for resources offered by other bodies

If you bid for resources from other local, national or international bodies, you will need to follow the same advice about establishing the criteria on which resources are allocated, and keeping to the criteria and the bidding format requested.

Costing a curriculum development proposal

When you propose a curriculum development or change, you should cost your proposal carefully so that you can secure the necessary resources to operate successfully. A curriculum development proposal should therefore include:

- an analysis of existing overall departmental staffing commitments
- minimum staffing requirements for the curriculum proposal, teaching time and staff experience

- minimum and maximum costs of any additional teaching time
- estimated running costs (stationery, books, equipment, reprographics)
- cost of any necessary staff INSET including supply teacher costs
- examination costs, including estimated supply teacher costs for moderation, orals, entry fees
- use of rooms and implications for room allocation of any specific course requirements, e.g. limit on group size, access to specialist equipment
- cost of any additional clerical/technician hours of support needed.

In addition, the 'opportunity' cost of the proposal needs to be considered. If the proposal is adopted, it may mean that other areas of development either within the department or within the school cannot go ahead. Equally the whole school may benefit from the opportunity if the proposal is adopted, e.g. increased recruitment into Year 12.

The following example together with the curriculum development forms may help.

ACTIVITY

The English department wishes to offer a new Drama examination course. This requires 4 periods of staff time per week for two years. There are two junior members of staff in their first year of teaching who are qualified to teach the course but both would need to attend a one-day course organised by the examining board. The course is held in October and will therefore probably involve supply teacher costs, together with the cost of travelling 50 miles by road to the course venue. There are four standard texts for the examination course costing £10.99, £9.99, £8.99 and £12.50. A number of reference texts would be helpful, and the department will have to purchase a set of stage lights, some stage make-up and will have to have some resources for production costs and for purchasing performing rights. It is anticipated that whole-school productions which develop out of the drama course will make some profit which can be re-invested into the course. The course will need to be based in

one of the bigger teaching rooms which will need to be adapted to become a drama studio. It will involve pupils in a 'production to an audience' which will require two days of supply cover. The cost of entering each pupil for the exam is £15.00. Initial responses from Year 9 pupils show that 15 pupils are interested in doing the course.

Calculate the approximate cost of this curriculum proposal.

What arguments could you use to convince the school's managers to allocate resources to this proposal?

Curriculum development proposal **RB25**

Subject

Head of Department

What is the title of the proposed course?	
Which exam board/organising body?	
Contact name/tel. no. for further information.	
What age range of pupils is the course intended for?	
What is the proposed start date for the course?	
What is the duration of the proposed course?	
Which (if any) course will be replaced by this course?	
What are the minimum and maximum pupil numbers for the viability of this proposal?	
What are the costs per pupil of exam entry?	
How many teaching periods will this proposal require?	
What will be the cost of this teaching commitment? (using an average cost of ___ per teaching period)	
Give names of existing staff who are qualified to teach this course.	
Will additional staff be needed to teach this course?	
What will be the implications for the rest of the courses taught by the department if this proposal is adopted?	

Signed ____________ Date ____________

Please give copies of this proposal to: ____________

nt **RB25**

Does the proposal include assessment arrangements which may involve the use of supply cover e.g. orals, aurals? Give details including proposed dates, supply teacher hours required and their cost.	
What are the approximate total costs of this proposal?	
Give reasons for proposing this curriculum development.	

Curriculum development proposal **RB26**

Subject

Name(s) of staff involved

Nature of proposed development

Age range

Examination Board/organising body

Date of proposed start

Staffing implications of proposed development
e.g. number of teaching periods required, staff who are qualified to teach proposed course, additional staffing required etc.

Resource implications of proposed change
e.g. accommodation, equipment, INSET, exam entry costs, teaching/learning materials, supply cover needed.

Total anticipated costs £

Justification for this curriculum development proposal
How will proposal help school to meet its aims, how will it be better than existing provision?

Discussed/Approved

There are photocopiable versions of these forms in the Resource Bank at the end of this book.

Monitoring resources

Once you have secured resources for your department you will need to monitor spending carefully and keep adequate records of purchases. Many schools now use computer-based systems which can provide a regular printout of money spent and committed.

You will want to ensure that there is a departmental system for allocating and retrieving the different teaching materials which staff require. It is important that this system is fair and is adhered to by all members of the department. A resource allocation form like the one opposite may be helpful for this exercise.

Resources allocation form RB9

Staff	Set	Term 1	Term 2	Term 3

There is a photocopiable version of this form in the Resource Bank at the end of this book.

You should:

- develop a system for allocating and retrieving resources allocated to pupils
- ensure that resources are stored securely
- check that members of the department have the necessary keys and use them.

Resource use can also be monitored by making it a reasonably regular item on the department team meeting agenda. This can be a useful forum for monitoring and discussing departmental spending on different areas of provision, e.g. for less able or more able pupils, A level, reprographics. Regular monitoring like this can ensure that there is overall balance and coherence in departmental use of resources as well as checking that there has been no over-spending.

Monitoring health and safety

As Head of Department, you have responsibilities for the health and safety of pupils and staff working within the departmental area. You will need to be aware of, and comply with, the relevant health and safety regulations. You should regularly monitor the health and safety aspects relating to the department's use of rooms and equipment and mode of operation.

The school will have:

- a designated health and safety officer
- published school guidelines on health and safety
- a procedure for reporting any accidents to staff or pupils
- a process for checking electrical equipment.

As Head of Department you should be vigilant and any problems must be reported promptly as equipment now has to be checked regularly. You should:

- ensure that suspect equipment is removed immediately
- check that emergency and fire safety notices are displayed in all departmental rooms
- ensure your staff are aware of the relevant procedures
- communicate relevant information to members of your department about any potentially dangerous medical conditions amongst your pupils, e.g. epilepsy, allergies, hearing loss.

Checklist for monitoring health and safety (RB10)

Do you know who the school's health and safety officer is?	Yes ☐ No ☐
Do you know of any specific health and safety matters relating to your department?	Yes ☐ No ☐
Is there a departmental policy for health and safety which is consistent with the overall school policy?	Yes ☐ No ☐
Are all members of your team aware of the health and safety policy?	Yes ☐ No ☐
Do members of your department team follow recommended health and safety procedures?	Yes ☐ No ☐
Do you regularly visually check all electrical items and report any suspected problems?	Yes ☐ No ☐
Do you know when was the last time electrical equipment was officially checked?	Yes ☐ No ☐
Do all teaching rooms have a clearly displayed fire notice?	Yes ☐ No ☐
Are fire exits clearly marked and do members of your department ensure that there is free access to them?	Yes ☐ No ☐
Do you know who is the nearest person in the school with medical/first aid training?	Yes ☐ No ☐
Have you got up-to-date lists of pupils' medical problems?	Yes ☐ No ☐
Are other staff in the department aware of these medical problems?	Yes ☐ No ☐
Do all members of the department know what to do in the event of an emergency?	Yes ☐ No ☐

There is a photocopiable version of this checklist in the Resource Bank at the end of this book.

Evaluation

It is important to evaluate the resources you have purchased and used in the preceding year. You should consider:

- how suitable they were for the purpose intended
- how well they stood up to the use to which they were put
- how well they helped you to meet your departmental priorities
- whether they provided value for money
- how well the pupils responded to them
- whether you should look for alternatives.

You should keep a collection of up-to-date publishers' catalogues and should send for inspection copies to circulate round the department throughout the year. This will mean that when it comes to the time for decisions about resources, you and your team will know what is currently available and whether they will suit your needs.

The efficiency of the management of the department can be judged by the extent to which resources are used to support and improve the standards of teaching and learning within the department. Good resource management can have an important impact on the quality of the educational outcomes from the department and contribute to the overall cost-effectiveness of the school. Resource management is therefore one of the key functions of a Head of Department.

5 Organising the department

Introduction

A newly appointed Head of Department once described her job as 'having 101 things to do and all at the same time'. As a Head of Department you will have a whole range of administrative tasks as well as managing the teaching/learning, resources and staff in your department. It is therefore important for Heads of Department to develop personal organisation skills.

Personal organisation

The necessary skills include:

- forward planning
- determining priorities
- managing time.

Forward planning

You will need to have a clear overview of the sequence of the school year and the needs of your department, e.g. for coursework or field trips. Departmental planners like the examples which follow can help you and your departmental team keep track of events. Photocopiable versions of these examples can be found in the Resource Bank at the end of this book.

Departmental planner

RB11

Month	To do: Details	Action	Completed

Departmental planner

RB12

Week no. & w/c	Department internal/ external coursework/ exams	Tutorial programme	School admin. meetings/parents' evenings	Visits, field trips, include work experience etc.	Sport and extra curricular activities	Assemblies

Using a daily personal planner can also help you to feel more in control of the conflicting demands on your time. There are photocopiable versions of these personal planners in the Resource Bank at the end of this book.

Personal planner

RB13

Subject	Action to be taken	Deadline	Follow-up

Daily planner

RB14

Date ____________________

Before school	**Notes**
Break	**Notes**
Lunch	**Notes**
After school	**Notes**

Priorities

This kind of planning can also be helpful for organising your thoughts about your priorities. You will need to decide what is:

- urgent and therefore needs immediate action
- important and needs to be done but does not call for immediate action
- long-term and needs some consideration
- information only and needs no further action.

Time management

Forward planning and prioritising help to produce effective time management. You should also consider:

- establishing routines, e.g. a set time each week to clear paperwork
- maintaining an orderly work place
- delegating responsibilities to others in the department
- making use of the school's clerical assistants for appropriate tasks.

Administration

Administration can occupy much of your time and you will need to consider:

- does it need to be done at all?
- when does this task need to be undertaken?
- when does this task need to be completed?
- what is the most efficient way of handling it?
- who should undertake this task?

The following list of common administration tasks is repeated in the *Administration tasks planner* in the Resource Bank in a format which may help you plan and organise your administration.

Administrative tasks

- preparation of departmental handbook, including schemes of work
- information to parents
- allocation of existing pupils to classes, sets
- examination preparation
- internal/external examination entries
- pupil assessment, recording and reporting
- pastoral care issues
- careers guidance and pupil placement
- staff induction
- staff development programme
- requisition and ordering
- stocktaking
- budget and finances
- health and safety
- primary/tertiary liaison
- special needs
- departmental statistical information
- parents' evenings
- departmental publicity
- non-teaching staff
- resources allocation.

Your task as Head of Department is to see that the work is distributed equitably between the members of your team and that it is done efficiently. A good manager is one who uses time, resources and people effectively.

Pupil records

Keeping pupil records is an important part of this administration. Pupil records include:

- set lists with staffing
- set changes throughout the year
- new pupils and set allocations
- examination entries
- examination results (internal and external)

- pupils with medical conditions
- pupils with special educational needs and referrals to the SENCO under the Code of Practice
- pupils referred to you by members of staff and action taken in relation to:
  - behaviour
  - lack of homework
  - recommendations for set changes
  - learning difficulties.

A referral form like the one below will help you to respond quickly to subsequent queries about pupils referred to you. A sample proforma is included in the Resource Bank at the end of the book.

Pupil referral form **RB16**

Pupil name	Reason for referral	Source of referral	Action	Date

Communication

Successful communication depends upon seeing that the right people (staff, parents, governors and pupils) have all the information they need, at the appropriate time and in a form they can absorb.

You need to consider:

- what you want to say
- how you want to say it (oral, written)
- who needs to know
- when they need to know.

Communication is most effective when it:

- is personal, ie. one to one
- is simple, direct, and fulfils a need or arouses interest
- is presented clearly in the appropriate form
- is conveyed at the correct and appropriate time.

Written communication can be an advantage or disadvantage in that:

- there is often a time difference between sending information and receiving a response (at times this can be useful)
- it can be retained as a record of the communication
- the sender is able to review the information and their message in order to convey the information adequately.

Oral communication should be used as a starting point wherever possible, especially if there is something disturbing, threatening or urgent to be communicated.

Meetings

At all levels within a school, meetings are one of the main methods of communicating. They can have many different functions, but their value depends on how well they are planned and managed. Meetings are normally held to fulfil one or more of the following purposes:

- to determine, approve or promote policies
- to plan future developments and decide on a course of action
- to exchange information
- to monitor and evaluate aspects of the department's work.

To conduct effective meetings you need to:

- allow enough time and plan in advance for important matters such as exams, syllabus planning, etc.
- circulate agendas and discussion papers in advance
- appoint a minute taker and make these minutes available to the department and to senior management
- deal with routine administrative matters by circular, mentioning them only briefly in the meeting. Meetings should deal with matters of educational importance and colleagues should feel that time is well spent

- give staff the opportunity to raise agenda items
- use meetings as in-service training sessions where appropriate, inviting members of the department to share expertise or work with colleagues with other responsibilities, e.g. the Special Needs Co-ordinator
- invite the Headteacher or Curriculum/Professional Development Deputy to attend where appropriate
- allocate some time for evaluation of work done, courses, resources, etc.
- celebrate success (exam results, etc.).

Communication with parents

You will need to keep parents and others fully informed about the courses and other opportunities offered by your department as well as informing parents about their child's progress. Communications should conform to a school or department style, look as professional as possible and be used consistently by all members of the department. Departmental communication may include:

- annual and termly reports
- information about the department for Open Evenings
- course information, e.g. GCSE, A level etc.
- coursework requirements
- subject-related careers/higher education opportunities
- standard letters to parents about
  - visits
  - homework
  - detentions
  - learning difficulties
  - loss of books
  - set/group allocation
  - set/group movement
  - pupil achievement.

It is important for the department's communications to create a positive impression. The following guidelines should help you:

- respond promptly and positively to all queries, requests or complaints
- ensure that all members of the department use the standard letters
- keep good records
- advise new staff about the writing of reports and the handling of parents' evenings
- monitor report writing within the department
- check that pupils' work is being marked regularly and according to departmental policy
- raise the status of your department within the school and the local community through displays, involvement of parents, extra-curricular activities, etc.
- listen to feedback from pupils and parents.

Liaison with other establishments

Regular communication with feeder schools and post-16 institutions is essential if there is to be continuity and progression in pupils' learning. Some schools have a large number of feeder schools and this can make regular personal contact difficult. However, it is important that feeder schools are kept informed about departmental developments and about the department's scheme of work. An annual subject meeting plus telephone contact about specific issues should be a minimum requirement. Other members of the department can be encouraged to take part in liaison arrangements. Also, it may be helpful to keep a record of liaison contacts so that there is *good* communication within the department and so that efforts are not duplicated. There is a photocopiable version of the record sheet which follows in the Resource Bank at the end of this book.

High School department liaison record **RB17**

Name of department ______________________

Date ______________ Member of staff ______________

Feeder school ______________________

Staff contacted ______________________

Reason for contact ______________________

Outcome of contact ______________________

Where school organisation cuts across a key stage of the curriculum, i.e. in a 13-18 high school, you will want to have more detailed discussions about the coverage of different aspects of the curriculum. There will also have to be agreement about assessment procedures and possibly about resources. It will be important to record and update such curriculum and assessment agreements regularly. A form like the KS3 continuity and progression form, RB18 in the Resource Bank can be helpful.

Contact with tertiary and higher education institutions will help you to be well informed about the educational options open to your pupils. Liaison should not only be about formal matters. Spending time in feeder schools, attending school and college open days, concerts or other activities all helps to build good relationships with colleagues and can help pupils at the point of transition. Inviting feeder-school staff and students into the department for specific curriculum activities can be particularly beneficial. There is a photocopiable version of the following checklist in the Resource Bank at the end of this book.

Checklist for good liaison with other establishments **RB19**

Have all feeder schools got copies of the department's schemes of work?	Yes ☐ No ☐
Has the department got copies of the feeder school's schemes of work?	Yes ☐ No ☐
Do all members of the department team know who are the relevant staff to contact in each feeder school?	Yes ☐ No ☐
Do all members of the department team know about post-16 educational options?	Yes ☐ No ☐
Is there an agreement with all feeder schools about the nature of assessment before transfer?	Yes ☐ No ☐
Is there agreement about the nature of subject-specific records, and evidence of achievement and how these will be passed on from feeder schools?	Yes ☐ No ☐
Have any members of the department visited feeder schools or post-16 institutions this term?	Yes ☐ No ☐
Have staff from feeder schools and/or post-16 institutions been invited to any department meeting or activity this term?	Yes ☐ No ☐
Are there plans for any joint curriculum development with feeder schools or post-16 institutions?	Yes ☐ No ☐

6 The department handbook

Introduction

The department handbook should be a record of all the essential information about the department. It should be a manageable and accessible source of information about the work of the department which can be used by other members of the department, new members of staff, senior managers, governors and inspectors. It will need to be updated every year and therefore a ring folder which allows for amendment and development is probably best.

A department handbook should contain:

- aims and objectives for the department
- schemes of work for all years and courses taught
- departmental policies
- the department's development plan
- resources available
- staff timetables
- staff qualifications, job descriptions, areas of responsibility within the department and record of in-service training
- non-teaching staff – hours of work, job descriptions, qualifications and record of in-service training
- health and safety records and procedures
- other documents relevant to the work of the department.

The department handbook should enable each member of the department to co-operate as a team, working within the broader context of the overall aims of the school.

A good test of its worth is to ask whether it would meet the needs of a colleague new to the school.

A useful way to start putting together a department handbook is to see what documentation and information already exists. Information about job descriptions or non-teaching staff hours of work and responsibilities may be held centrally in the school. Exam syllabuses can be obtained from the exam boards and may have useful lists of aims and objectives which can be adapted to wider contexts. Other department heads may have useful documents. The following checklist may help to get you started. There is a photocopiable version of it in the Resource Bank at the end of this book.

Checklist for writing a department handbook

RB20

Do I have an up-to-date copy of the school's aims?		Yes ☐	No ☐
Do I have copies of exam board syllabuses?		Yes ☐	No ☐
Has the department got up-to-date aims and objectives?		Yes ☐	No ☐
Have I got copies of any departmental policies?		Yes ☐	No ☐
Are there detailed schemes of work for all courses taught in the department?		Yes ☐	No ☐
Has the department got a development plan?		Yes ☐	No ☐
Have I got details about the resources available?		Yes ☐	No ☐
Have I got details of:	staff qualifications?	Yes ☐	No ☐
	recent INSET?	Yes ☐	No ☐
	job descriptions?	Yes ☐	No ☐
	areas of responsibility?	Yes ☐	No ☐
	teaching commitment?	Yes ☐	No ☐
Have I got details of:	non-teaching staff hours?	Yes ☐	No ☐
	job descriptions?	Yes ☐	No ☐
	qualifications?	Yes ☐	No ☐
	recent INSET?	Yes ☐	No ☐
Do I have information about health and safety procedures in the department?		Yes ☐	No ☐

The department's aims and objectives

Before thinking in detail about the department's aims and objectives you should be clear about what and how the department wishes pupils to learn. You also need to think about the overall learning environment in which the department is operating. There are three main aspects which need to be considered:

1 **The School – its structure and overall curriculum**

- overall aims and objectives
- curriculum progression and continuity: pre-11 to post-16
- curriculum content of other related areas, e.g. PSE
- cross-curricular links
- pupil intake – abilities, social attitudes, cultural background
- equal opportunities
- timetabling policy, structures, constraints, pupil groupings
- overall streaming and classroom provision
- financial situation
- non-teaching support
- appraisal and staff development policy
- assessment, recording and reporting policy.

2 **The Department – subject area and team of staff**

- subject aims and objectives
- course content – skills, knowledge and understanding
- classroom facilities and layout
- teaching skills – strengths and weaknesses of team
- books, materials, equipment and resources
- deployment of non-teaching staff
- teaching methods
- staff development and appraisal
- assessment, recording and reporting.

3 External influences – and new initiatives

- external advice and support
- DFEE initiatives
- TEC initiatives
- exam boards and syllabuses
- National Curriculum
- National Record of Achievement
- other national and local initiatives and arrangements.

The aims of the department should be expressed in a straightforward way. Start by asking the following questions:

- What are we trying to achieve by teaching this subject to pupils?
- Why is the subject important?
- What will it add to the pupils' understanding of the world in which they live?
- How could it help them in the future?

The department's aims should refer to, and support, the school's overall aims.

EXAMPLE OF DEPARTMENTAL AIMS

History Department

The study of History supports the school's overall aims of enabling students to develop tolerance and understanding of others as well as preparing them for life and work in the 21st century. The aims of the History Department are to enable students to:

- develop knowledge and understanding of people in the past and how they lived their lives
- explore concepts of causation, continuity and change
- understand how the past shapes the present
- learn historical skills of analysis, comparison, and synthesis which are also relevant to employment in the future
- develop qualities of scepticism, empathy and imagination.

Objectives

These are statements about specific, measurable outcomes which are derived from your aims. For example:

- **To be able to describe some of the causes and consequences of the 2nd World War**
- **To be able to put events in date order**

The scheme of work

These are essential documents as they itemise the learning and assessment experiences pupils are to receive. As such, however, they will need to be prepared for a wide audience. It is helpful to produce them at two levels:

1 **In outline:**

for senior staff
other departments/faculties
parents
pupils
governors

This is essentially for quick and accessible reference to information about the department as part of the school's overall curriculum statement. It should, therefore:

- identify for each group/course the key ideas, themes, areas of knowledge and understanding, and skills to be developed
- be short and concise
- be free of jargon
- make use of simple flow charts to express ideas where possible
- refer to any timetabling structure, e.g. group rotation
- be clearly and attractively laid out, with subdivisions for ease of reference.

The outline scheme of work should provide a summary of how the department intends to deliver its planned curriculum for pupils.

2 In detail:

This is for those actually doing the teaching. As this is an 'operators' manual' it will need to give a week-by-week breakdown of the course content, identifying:

- the key ideas, areas of knowledge and understanding and skills to be developed
- how it relates to the National Curriculum programmes of study
- pupils' activities and suggested teaching methods
- the resources that could or should be used
- any details of group rotation and other aspects of the structure
- details of aspects of learning to be assessed and appropriate criteria and methods
- the progression between previous and future work (including pre- and post-secondary)
- any cross-curricular links, and relationship to courses in any other subjects
- opportunities for differentiation between pupils of differing abilities, including extension work
- issues such as equal opportunities, multi-cultural awareness and social attitudes.

Writing schemes of work to cover all these elements can seem daunting. It is useful to start with an outline scheme and then add more detail to it. It can also be helpful to plan the scheme of work using a planning grid to ensure that all the elements are covered. Photocopiable versions of the sample planning grids opposite are included in the Resource Bank at the end of this book.

Remember to ask others in the department to take a share in writing the department's scheme of work. It is best, however, to agree first on a common format.

Planning grid for scheme of work RB21

Topic:	Stage:		Year:	
Key questions	Concepts/terminology	Teaching & learning	Resources	Homework

Planning grid for scheme of work RB22

Topic:			Lesson:		
Content	Resources	Core	Extension work for most able	Approach for less able	Homework

Planning grid for scheme of work RB23

	Content	Resource	Task	Pupil outcome	Teacher response
Level 1–3					
Level 3–6					

Choosing a syllabus

When writing your scheme of work you may want to review the department's choice of exam syllabus especially as the choice of syllabus may affect the number of exam passes. Consider the following checklist. There is a photocopiable version of it in the Resource Bank at the end of this book.

Checklist for choosing a syllabus RB24

Is there a good match between the expertise of the department and the demands of the syllabus?	Yes ☐	No ☐
Are the exam results with this syllabus satisfactory?	Yes ☐	No ☐
Is the balance between coursework and final assessment satisfactory?	Yes ☐	No ☐
Are other syllabuses available?	Yes ☐	No ☐
Do members of the department have experience of teaching other syllabuses?	Yes ☐	No ☐
Have students expressed any preferences about the syllabus?	Yes ☐	No ☐
Would there be any resource implications in changing the syllabus?	Yes ☐	No ☐

In deciding whether to change a syllabus you may need to:

- contact various exam boards and become familiar with what is available
- build up a 'library for you and your colleagues' for reference purposes
- consult widely on the merits of particular syllabuses including other schools
- ensure that the syllabuses will meet your needs for some years to come and are compatible with local and national developments, especially if heavy investment of time and resources are required
- choose the one(s) that best meets your aims and objectives and teaching skills after full consultation with your team
- prepare a realistic timescale for implementation, and delegate the preparation of units wherever possible.

Developing departmental policies

A policy is a statement of intent, but it is more effective if it states how intentions are put into practice.

The policy should describe the means whereby particular objectives are to be realised.

Department policies should, where appropriate, make reference to and be coherent with whole-school policy statements. In addition, they should reflect what is actually happening.

Department policies might include:

- assessment, recording and reporting
- marking
- exam entry
- differentiation
- teaching methods
- equal opportunities
- homework
- groupings of pupils
- information technology
- special needs, including the more able
- liaison with other schools, other departments
- cross-curricular skills including problem solving, study skills, oracy
- cross-curricular themes
- rewards and sanctions
- behaviour
- multi-cultural awareness
- extra-curricular activities.

Writing a departmental policy

It is important to stress that you do not have to re-invent the wheel or write lengthy philosophical statements.

You should begin by checking whether there is a whole-school policy for the area under consideration. If there is, it is important that your department's statement supports the school's policy. If there isn't, you may want to begin by collecting examples of good practice from other departments, other schools or external advisers. These can provide a starting point for discussion with your colleagues.

The following flow diagram may be helpful to show how departmental policies can be formulated.

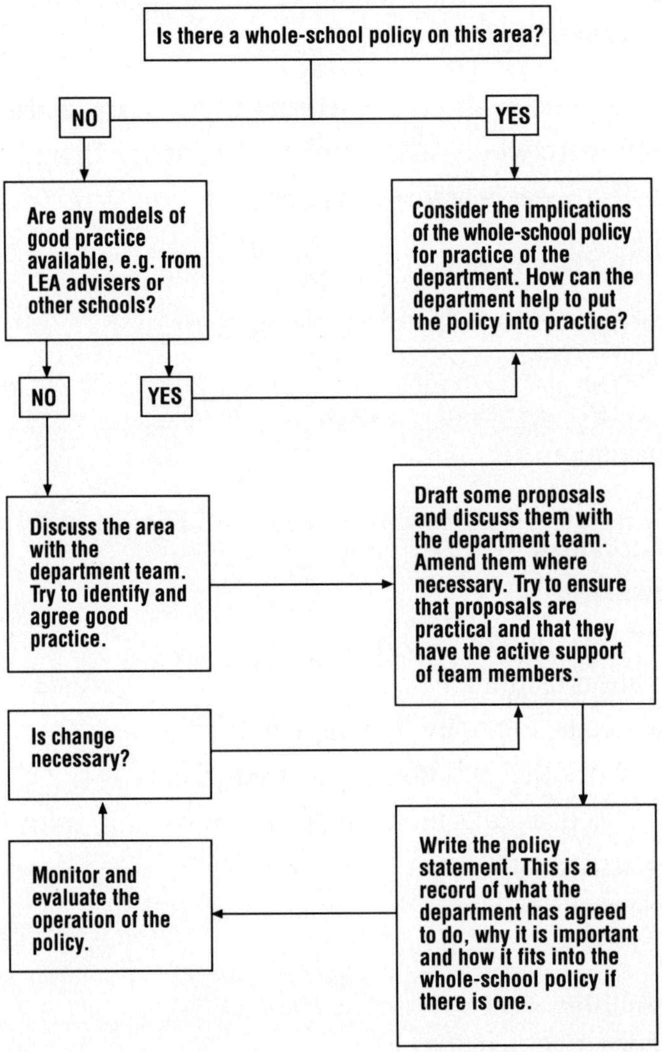

Activity

Consider the following guidelines on assessment and marking and any whole-school policies your school has. Write your own departmental assessment policy.

Sample departmental policies

A: Assessment and marking guidelines

1. THE NATURE OF ASSESSMENT

1.1 The term assessment is taken here to mean any evaluative observation or measurement of the performance of individual pupils, or groups of pupils, in any aspect of educational provision made by the school.

1.2 A synthesis of the purposes of assessment is:

a) Diagnosis-
to monitor progress and to discover how a given pupil is assimilating what is being taught. Specific action may be instituted as a result of diagnostic assessment.

b) Evaluation -
to judge the effectiveness of the teaching and learning which again can lead to specific action.

c) Formative -
to provide ongoing information for pupil and teacher to decide how learning should be advanced, identify strengths and weaknesses, help diagnostic processes, etc.

d) Grading -
to differentiate between the work of individual students, to assign pupils to a particular group.

e) Guidance -
to assist pupils to make decisions about performance, subjects or courses and careers.

f) Information -
to assist in communication with parents, governing bodies and the wider community about the achievements of pupils in school.

g) Prediction -
to discover potential abilities and aptitudes and to predict probable successes whether in school or elsewhere.

h) Selection -
to determine suitability for courses, classes, Higher Education, etc.

i) Summation -
to provide overall evidence of the achievements of a pupil and the extent of skills, knowledge and understanding.

1.3 So, assessment embraces not only formal examinations, testing, etc., but also teacher response to written assignments, oral questioning, contribution to group work as well as observation of pupil interest, attitude and effort. It includes perceptive, subjective judgements based on professional experience and knowledge. Assessment is an essential element in any teaching strategy and is as much concerned with providing positive, supportive response to pupils' work as with awarding marks or grades.

Structured and guided self- and peer-assessment are also valid as part of a total assessment package.

1.4 The overall purpose of assessment is to promote pupil learning, leading to higher achievement by providing motivation to learn. Many of the preceding aspects of assessment require follow-up action if improved learning is to be the outcome, e.g. changes in the learning process, remedial help, additional stimulus, transfer between groups. Examinations and tests offer a focus for study and clearly defined goals, providing an incentive to effort. Other less formal assessments involving a supportive and constructive appraisal of pupils' day-to-day work also provide motivation for further endeavour by placing value on pupils' work and indicating that there are high expectations of the individual. Motivation is strongest when a reasonable degree of success is achieved. Assessment resulting in frequent failure damages pupils' self esteem and confidence and is likely to act as a disincentive to an interest in learning.

1.5 There are broadly two groups of reasons for assessment: those concerned with helping the pupil and those concerned with assisting the teacher. Both are dynamic and involve interacting with the evaluation of the curriculum and teaching and learning styles. Assessment can help to:

a) gather information about a wide range of pupil characteristics as feedback for making decisions
b) accumulate records of progress
c) provide information from which teachers can obtain insights into their own effectiveness
d) compare success of different teaching and learning styles
e) provide information for other teachers who have to make decisions about pupils
f) compare new teaching materials with those previously used
g) make decisions about the curriculum as a whole, e.g. introduction of new courses
h) provide incentives to learn and an aid to memory
i) compare the progress of pupils with different teachers
j) allocate pupils to sets
k) inform parents about progress
l) inform employers or other educational establishments about attainment
m) decide whether pupils will be entered for external examinations.

1.6 A whole-school assessment policy should be based on the following major principles:

a) assessment should be positive in nature, as far as possible, in order to motivate and encourage pupils
b) assessment should be integral to the teaching philosophy and taught curriculum
c) assessment needs to be supportive, formative and diagnostic, and to identify specific skills and abilities
d) assessment should enable suitable remedial and extension work to be put into place
e) a variety of different assessment procedures, including formal and common assessment, should be utilised. Methods chosen should be appropriate with regard to the reason for the assessment and type of information being sought
f) the purpose, nature and outcome of assessment and grading systems used should be clear and communicated to pupils, parents and other staff in an unambiguous way.

1.7 Assessment, therefore, is fundamental to all aspects of school life: academic or pastoral distinctions become blurred as they strive to the same end.

2. ASSESSMENT PROCEDURES

2.1 Assessment procedures must be the subject of regular review if they are to fulfil successfully the overall aims and objectives of the school, meet changing curricular demands and satisfy the specific objectives of the assessment programme. For assessment to be worthwhile, it should be an integral part of the teaching/learning process and include formal and informal feedback. Present formal arrangements allow for classwork marking, homework (and homework diaries), tests, examinations and reports. Departments must ensure that such efforts fulfil the whole-school policy needs, departmental objectives and the broader assessment purposes detailed in section 1. All interested parties should be aware of what is being assessed, how and why. Otherwise there may be a conflict of interests, repetition or unnecessary expenditure of time, resources and energy.

2.2 The assessment of an individual's performance is increasingly being made by comparison with pre-determined criteria. The criterion referenced task is designed to establish whether particular standards, skills, understanding, etc., have been grasped. Criterion referenced assessment used predetermined levels of performance, assessment being made in relation to objectives. This has the advantage that criteria can be pitched at any level, and, given sufficient sophistication of task, be tailored to the individual for diagnostic or feedback purposes. A scheme of work which involves criterion referencing should adequately delineate skills, knowledge, and application of principles. It will relate to the learning process and not be concerned solely with the learning product.

2.3 Comparisons between individuals are sometimes necessary. Such norm referencing has the major disadvantage that by differentiating between individuals, failure is liable to be reinforced. Norm referencing does not establish, per se, any externalised concepts of standards. Norm referenced tests are discrimination tests which aim to discover how much each pupil has benefited from the course. It achieves a 'rank order' of pupils in terms of test measured ability.

2.4 It is also possible to measure pupils against their own previous performance. Such assessment is more dynamic in that it will change in conformity with a pupil's level of performance. Assessment tends in practice to involve elements of both norm – and criterion – referencing.

2.5 Subject departments need to ensure that changing curricula have an integrated assessment programme which allows for criterion referencing as well as norm referencing. It is essentially important to consider approaches to assessment when designing differentiated tasks. Such programmes need:

a) changes in methodology
b) changes in content
c) changes in style of testing/examining
d) greater emphasis on continuous assessment
e) development of criterion referenced assessment
f) record of achievement and self-assessment.

3. MARKING POLICY

3.1 It is fundamentally important that marking is frequent, consistent and helpful. It is not always necessary to close mark the whole of every pupil's exercise every time. Each department should have a marking policy in place, a copy of which should be submitted to the Headteacher. The policy should:

a) ensure a common approach across a Department
b) ensure the Heads of Department have an overall view of what is being covered in the department
c) ensure that marking is regular
d) provide an appraisal of pupils' work and progress
e) encourage and involve pupils, especially those who may be underachieving, by providing supportive guidelines for improvement
f) ensure that parents are aware of the existence of a policy and encourage them to respond and participate.

3.2 The policy should be:

a) as straightforward and simple as possible so that all parties involved understand it
b) constructive and in the interests of the pupils
c) practical and effective to avoid overburdening staff
d) consistent across the school, yet flexible enough to answer specific subject needs.

3.3 Marking procedures should cover content, effort and presentation. The marking/grading system should be agreed and used across a department and consistently applied. Numbers and letters do very similar things. They state how much a piece of work falls short of perfection – for a child of that particular age and ability being assessed on particular skills/knowledge etc. Above all, the pupil must be absolutely clear what it is that her/his mark represents.

3.4 Occasionally exercises will require no more than a tick, but at least this will indicate that the work has received the scrutiny of the teacher. Follow-up can be made on subsequent work. Most exercises require and merit a more careful, in-depth examination and to be commented upon as a minimum – and frequently will also be given a mark/grade.

3.5 Comments are welcomed by pupils and should praise content and effort where possible – with specific reference to what has been done well. Direction and specific assistance should be given to aid improvement. Comments help to build up a more personal rapport between pupil and teacher. A comment should be:

a) legible to the pupil
b) intelligible to the pupil
c) useful
d) constructive and/or positive.

3.6 It is envisaged that 'close scrutiny' marking of work should take place approximately once every three weeks. Thus, over a period of a school year, a pupil would have received such treatment at least ten times. The work of certain pupils would benefit from close scrutiny more often. Work should be marked and returned promptly. Comments/marks/grades become less meaningful to pupils if a long period of time elapses between collection and return of classwork/homework.

3.7 Self- and peer-marking are valid exercises as an aspect of the whole teaching and learning/assessment package. This approach can provide pupils with instant feedback and an insight into why and how marking takes place and so aid understanding of what is required in work being covered.

3.8 Presentation should be in line with an agreed, consistent departmental policy for all age and ability levels. A common standard of presentation should be arrived at, e.g. new work should be titled, title underlined and dated; finished work should be ruled off, etc.

3.9 It may be worthwhile to give a separate grade/mark for effort/presentation and utilise the Reward System to encourage positive attitudes. In similar vein to the subject reports, departments may decide to include effort/presentation as part of the criteria of assessment pieces/programme.

Untidy work, poorly maintained books and graffiti should be discouraged at all times. Action should be taken with pupils whose work is consistently good/bad over a given period.

Commendations should be noted in the homework diary and a tutor slip could be filled in to encourage achievement further.

A subject teacher should first inform parents of poor work by noting shortcomings in the pupil's homework diary. Persistent problems should be referred to the Head of Department and if there is still no improvement a tutor slip should be given to the Head of Year, appropriate joint action taken and the slip put on file.

B: Equal Opportunities

EQUAL OPPORTUNITIES IN MATHEMATICS

It is the aim of this department to maximise the potential of all pupils in its care. To seek to ensure that this objective is met the department is conscious that certain groups may suffer disadvantages due to disability, or difference in gender or ethnic origin.

In mathematics, research has shown that this can be seen as a 'male' subject. There are many areas in which disadvantage can consciously or unconsciously occur, and the department notes the need to attend to the concept of equal opportunities in general, and to each of the following points in particular.

<u>Lesson content:</u> Members of the department are made aware of the need to ensure that they make every effort to avoid bias in their lessons by including examples which can be related to all members of society. Where this is impractical, staff should include a balance of examples.

<u>Books and materials:</u> Classroom materials can fail to indicate the multicultural nature of society, and also may give an untrue view of the role of women in the modern world, both of which would give a false impression to pupils. The department accepts the need to regularly monitor books and materials in use in the classroom. However those currently used (SMP 11-16) are widely held to be excellent in this regard.

<u>Staffing:</u> In a subject which is widely held to be 'male' orientated, an imbalance in the number and role of members of staff can reinforce this viewpoint. While there have been times when there have been significantly more male teachers than female, or more female teachers than male, in this subject, over time this has levelled out (although appointment has always been made on merit).

Optional courses: The department is aware that fewer female students than male students opt for the subject in Years 12 and 13 nationally. Whilst this is also true within this school there has been an increase in the proportion of female students who have been successful in the subject at 'A' level in recent years. The department is actively seeking ways of improving the range of courses offered in Years 12 and 13 with a view to offering syllabuses which are more attuned to all potential sixth formers. With this in mind GCSE Statistics was offered as a one year course recently and the introduction of a modular 'A' and 'A/S' course should enable the department to once again offer Statistics as an option.

Information Technology: Many concepts in mathematics can profitably be taught through the medium of Information Technology (as indicated in the National Curriculum). The department wholeheartedly supports the I.T. Equal Opportunities policy and will support its aim of enabling equality of access.

C: Special Needs

The department is aware of its responsibilities under the Code of Practice and works with the SEN Co-ordinator to identify and support pupils with Special Educational Needs.

The department has a representative on the School's Learning Support Team which meets every 2 weeks.

Support includes:

- specialist in-class support where possible and appropriate
- use of Y12 pupil volunteers as 'classroom assistants'
- reducing the number of pupils in certain groups to allow more individual attention
- the use of differentiated teaching materials and methods.

The department also recognises the special needs of more able pupils and seeks to challenge them both through extension work and enrichment activities.

The progress of all pupils including those with special educational needs is monitored through assessment, observation and discussion at departmental meetings.

D: Rewards

The Science Department supports the whole-school policy of rewarding pupils' achievement and effort at all levels of ability. We believe that it is important to emphasise pupil's achievements, to celebrate their success and to involve their parents whenever possible in this. The Science Department's policy is to:

- display pupils' work wherever possible, making sure that it represents work from the whole range of ability
- award merit marks for work (written, oral, practical, etc.) which demonstrates achievement within the set or which demonstrates particular effort or commitment
- award a letter home to parents commending the pupil's effort/achievement where a pupil receives 5 merits in a term
- award a certificate and a letter home to parents commending the pupil's effort/achievement where a pupil receives 10 merits in a term.

E: Sanctions

The Maths Department operates a policy on sanctions in line with the whole-school policy on pupil behaviour. This means the use of staged sanctions to deal with misbehaviour in the classroom and the involvement of parents at an early stage of any pattern of misbehaviour.

stage 1 – clear verbal warning that the behaviour is unacceptable
stage 2 – pupil moved to another place in the classroom
stage 3 – pupil put outside the door for a short period so that the teacher can have a private word to emphasise that the behaviour is unacceptable. The teacher will also fill in a referral form to notify the form tutor and year head at this stage
stage 4 – lunchtime or evening detention. Parents must be informed and a departmental detention letter must be sent giving the parents 24 hours' notice of the detention and the reason for it. A copy of this letter must be given to the Head of Department so that records can be kept.

In the case of more serious misbehaviour, the head of year must be involved. The head of year also has a range of sanctions which can be used, e.g. daily report card, head of year detention, temporary isolation, etc. It is also important for the head of year to be informed of persistent misbehaviour as it may be necessary to assess the student for stage 1 of the Code of Practice (where behavioural problems are hindering learning). The members of the department take it in turns to operate a department detention on Thursday nights for pupils who have failed to complete homework or classwork without an appropriate reason.

7 Preparing for OFSTED inspection

Introduction

All schools are now inspected by the Office for Standards in Education (OFSTED). The 1992 Education Act requires registered inspectors to use a standard framework to report on:

- the quality of education provided by the school
- the educational standards achieved by the school
- whether the financial resources made available to the school are managed effectively
- the spiritual, moral and cultural development of students.

'The central purpose of the report is to communicate clearly and effectively, to an audience which should be taken to consist largely of non-professionals who need to be able to see at once, without reading between lines, the strengths and weaknesses of the school, its overall quality, the standards pupils are achieving, and what should be done if improvements are needed.'

(OFSTED)

The Head of Department is responsible for the quality of teaching and learning within the department and for ensuring that the department is fully prepared for the inspection.

Departmental documentation

Inspectors will require documentation from a department prior to an inspection. Inspectors are instructed to assess whether:

'Values, plans and procedures (are) expressed in clear policies and documentation.'

(Framework of OFSTED Inspection 1992)

Policies and procedures

Inspectors will want to ensure that departmental policies are formulated within the context of whole-school policies and that practice and procedures match what is claimed in the documentation. For example:

Special Educational Needs

- Is the department's policy coherent with the whole-school policy?
- What provision does the department make for students with special needs?
- Does the department's provision and practice maximise the access of students with special needs to the curriculum?

Equal Opportunities

- Is the department's policy coherent with the whole-school policy?
- Do teachers understand how factors such as ethnicity, gender and social circumstance may affect learning?
- Does the department have an active monitoring system?
- Are resources monitored for bias?
- Is a positive image of women and ethnic minorities presented?
- Do teaching strategies and student groupings avoid bias?

Other possible policy areas

- primary, secondary and post-16 liaison
- discipline and rewards
- health and safety

- the library
- school–industry links and the work-related curriculum
- charging for school trips
- communicating with parents
- use of displays
- dissemination of information about careers opportunities within the subject
- staff development
- assessment (including recording, reporting and marking).

The development plan

The department's development plan will be required and it should contain clear objectives and costed, attainable targets.

Documentation required

Inspectors will be particularly interested in the department's scheme of work and the extent to which documentation explains:

- how work is arranged if teachers are absent
- arrangements for the ordering of stock and resources
- details of how technicians, support staff and unqualified staff are managed
- details of departmental resources stating which are to be used with which year groups
- use and rotation of classrooms.

They will also wish to see details of department procedures. For example:

- a list of members of the department, detailing their agreed responsibilities within the department
- methods of communication and consultation within the department
- how the department's performance and procedures are reviewed and evaluated and its members appraised
- the ways in which teaching, standards of student's achievement, marking and assessment are regularly monitored.

It is helpful and looks professional to collate all this documentation in a departmental handbook so that it can be presented to inspectors. However the departmental handbook should be primarily a working manual which members of the department can use and refer to.

The management of the department

Inspectors will look for evidence that the Head of Department is:

- managing the department effectively and efficiently
- publicising the department's aims and translating them into clear objectives and attainable targets
- establishing priorities for development based on sound evaluation
- ensuring the development and training of staff is clearly linked to their responsibilities
- ensuring that pupils and staff understand what is expected of them
- ensuring that communication lines are clearly understood and utilised
- promoting an orderly environment, positive attitudes to work and sound relationships
- managing finance efficiently and focusing it on clear priorities
- keeping parents and others well-informed about children's progress
- undertaking a systematic review of the schemes of work
- monitoring their implementation
- evaluating the outcomes for pupils.

Key responsibilities

The Head of Department's main responsibilities are listed opposite. Some key considerations that inspectors will look for are included.

Leadership and direction

- Leading the department to a common goal
- Devising the department's development plan in collaboration with colleagues
- Devising the departmental handbook and the scheme of work.

Curriculum management

- Setting high expectations
- Organising and motivating people to get things done effectively and efficiently
- Taking an overview of the subject curriculum and relating it to the whole curriculum.

Curriculum evaluation

- Devising a planned programme for evaluating schemes of work
- Devising a planned programme for evaluating children's experience.

Management of teaching and learning

- Influencing methodology and teaching styles
- Monitoring and maintaining standards of teaching and learning
- Pupil grouping.

Assessment, recording and reporting

- Devising procedures for assessment, recording and reporting.

Monitoring staff

- Monitoring and assessing the work of staff using agreed job descriptions, targets and performance indicators
- Devising and assigning formal roles.

Administration

- Devising and implementing methods of operation and administrative procedures.

Appraisal and staff development

- Appraising staff
- Ensuring staff development, including inducting newly qualified teachers, new staff and supervising students.

Communication

- Communicating school policy to the department
- Communicating departmental policy to the department

- Communicating from the department to the Senior Management Team
- Management consultation and meetings within the department.

Management of relationships

- Relationships with SMT (curriculum, timetable, etc.)
- Relationships with other Heads of Department
- Team building
- Delegating
- Managing formal and informal relationships with and between colleges
- Pastoral care of colleagues.

Management of resources

- Managing the budget, learning resources
- Assigning appropriate resources for all pupils of all ages and abilities
- Ensuring equal opportunities (gender, ethnicity) taken into account in choice of resources
- Ensuring library contains books relating to department curriculum area
- Ensuring use made of external resources, e.g. museums, local environment
- Monitoring health and safety, e.g. COSHH regulations
- Deploying staff
- Managing support staff.

Management of accommodation

Ensuring:

- Rooms suit co-operative working
- Rotation of rooms to benefit pupils, not for staff convenience
- Furniture clean, rooms tidy and welcoming
- Desks free of graffiti
- Sufficient storage space for pupils' equipment.

Management of display

Ensuring:

- Equal opportunities (gender, ethnicity) taken into account
- Mix of pupils' and commercially produced material

- Work from pupils of all abilities
- Display interactive with the curriculum, e.g. contains technical vocabulary.

Setting an example of professionalism

- Teaching in a highly competent manner
- Ensuring instructional leadership (do what I do, not do as I say)
- Keeping up to date.

Cross-phase liaison

- Meeting with partner primary schools and post-16 institutions
- Ensuring liaison is curriculum-based, not only pastoral
- Organising teacher exchange
- Arranging joint moderation of National Curriculum assessment.

Appointing staff

- Participating in the appointments procedure.

Communicating with parents

Ensuring:

- Parents understand the school's aims and who it intends to achieve them
- Written information to parents (newsletters, prospectus, etc.) is clear, frequent and jargon free
- Frequent parents' meetings
- Reports to parents provide statutory information
- Pupils' files contain parental correspondence and appropriate responses to parental enquiries and complaints
- Parents welcome in the school, involvement in life of school, and work as helpers.

Management of external relationships

- Relationships with external agencies.

Promoting the department

- Promoting the department positively within the school but not to the detriment of others.

Discipline and rewards

- Taking an active role in practising policies for rewards and discipline
- Establishing departmental sanctions.

Extra-curricular activities

- Encouraging extra-curricular activities.

Inspection and the classroom

This section examines what inspectors will be looking for when they carry out classroom observation. The main points set out below provide a checklist for department members.

Accommodation and resources

- Accommodation, all equipment, materials safe
- Room tidy, welcoming, good display
- Resources in good condition and accessible.

Preparation

- Teacher on time to lesson
- Pupils arrive in an orderly manner
- Register taken
- Homework marked with positive comments and good follow-up.

Planning

- Good quality, sufficient, differentiated and appropriate resources
- Lesson has clear purpose which is communicated by the teachers and understood by the pupils
- Lesson has clear target of what pupils should have achieved by the end of the lesson
- Activities varied and reflect the target for the lesson
- Lesson plan in evidence.

Teaching

- Scheme of work being followed

- Content and teaching style appropriate to age and ability of pupils
- All pupils challenged, involved in lesson, able to achieve success
- Questioning appropriate, and extended replies encouraged
- Differentiated
- Expectations high
- Lesson has pace.

Pupils' response

- Pupils working on task
- Pupils understanding the tasks and the reasons for doing them
- Pupils perceiving the work to be relevant, challenging and interesting
- Pupils participating actively and thinking for themselves
- Pupils enjoying the work.

Relationships

- Good relationships in the classroom between pupils and pupil and teacher
- Good standards of behaviour and co-operation
- Pupils depart in orderly manner.

Standard of achievement

- The extent of knowledge, understanding and skills acquired by pupils in relation to Attainment Targets and Programmes of Study
- Pupils' competence in reading, writing, oracy, listening and numeracy. Quality of work in lesson and in books related to pupils' age and ability. Special circumstances which may have affected students' standards of achievement.

Quality of learning

- Pupils' competence as learners
- Reading, writing, listening, talking and numeracy
- Observation, seeking information, seeking patterns and deeper understanding, posing questions, discussing alternatives, solving problems, applying what has been learned to unfamiliar situations, evaluating work done
- Ability to co-operate, work productively with others
- Ability to concentrate, work at appropriate pace
- Gains in knowledge, understanding and skills in the lesson.

Quality of teaching

- Command of subject content
- Planning: clear goals for group and individuals, range of activities, suitability of content, effective use of resources, appropriateness of pace for all
- Classroom organisation: pupil groupings, display, role of support staff and relationship to specialist
- Marking, comments and follow-up
- Teacher records of work, arrangements to improve teaching
- Contribution to key skills.

Action Planning

The report produced by the inspection team will raise KEY ISSUES to which the governing body must respond via a published action plan. The key issues will contain, amongst other things, those aspects of the school's provision which do not meet with statutory requirements and/or health and safety standards. There may be implications in the key issues section for one, some or all departments. For example:

'... raise levels of achievement and develop pupils' learning skills across all curriculum areas.'

'... at key stage 3 in art, PE and music the schemes of work pay insufficient attention to the needs of pupils with learning difficulties.'

'... set goals for the improvement of pupils' achievements in science with particular attention to the pace of their learning and the level of challenge especially at KS3.'

Even if the key issues section has few or no implications for curriculum areas, each Head of Department will find it extremely useful to scrutinise the report written on his/her area(s). A significant amount of detail is contained in the report based on a substantial evidence base of observation, discussion, scrutiny of pupils' work, analysis of documentation, etc. By taking the following steps Heads of Department will be able to develop an action plan which addresses the issues to emerge from the report in a systematic way:

Steps in Action Planning

1. Read the report several times and either list 'strengths' and 'weaknesses' or carry out a **SWOT** analysis – **S**trengths, **W**eaknesses, **O**pportunities and **T**hreats. This exercise will offer you a swift, overall view of what the inspectors thought about your department.
2. Share your findings with other colleagues from the department or indeed carry out the exercise as a team.
3. Agree your priorities. Consider whether some of the issues are part of your development plan anyway. Decide whether they should be replaced or restated in the light of the issues raised by the inspectors.
4. Select ONE issue at a time and outline the tasks needed to tackle it.
5. Decide on the precise action to be taken.
6. Ensure that your plan is achievable and realistic.
7. Set a deadline for the action.
8. Identify the resources needed e.g. personnel from within or outside the school, time, money, equipment.
9. Name the person(s) responsible for ensuring that the agreed action is taken.
10. State how progress in tackling the issues will be monitored, whose responsibility it is and in what form they should report.

    - What needs to be done?
    - What are the criteria for achievement?
    - Who is responsible for which task?
    - How will the task be dealt with?
    - When will the action be completed?
    - What resources will be required?
    - How will progress be gauged?

There are some photocopiable formats, to help you structure your Action Planning in the Resource Bank at the end of this book.

Resource Bank

Self evaluation questionnaire

RB1

Rate your performance using the scale:
1 = very good 2 = good 3 = satisfactory 4 = some weakness 5 = area for improvement

Be honest with yourself – and don't underestimate your abilities!

1 Ability to communicate with members of the department team	1 ☐	2 ☐	3 ☐	4 ☐	5 ☐
2 Ability to communicate ideas in writing	1 ☐	2 ☐	3 ☐	4 ☐	5 ☐
3 Ability to communicate ideas orally	1 ☐	2 ☐	3 ☐	4 ☐	5 ☐
4 Ability to represent the views of the department team to the Senior Management	1 ☐	2 ☐	3 ☐	4 ☐	5 ☐
5 Ability to represent the views of the Senior Management Team to the department	1 ☐	2 ☐	3 ☐	4 ☐	5 ☐
6 Ability to organise the administrative work of the department	1 ☐	2 ☐	3 ☐	4 ☐	5 ☐
7 Ability to delegate responsibilities to others in the department team	1 ☐	2 ☐	3 ☐	4 ☐	5 ☐
8 Ability to chair departmental meetings	1 ☐	2 ☐	3 ☐	4 ☐	5 ☐
9 Ability to handle difficult members of the department	1 ☐	2 ☐	3 ☐	4 ☐	5 ☐
10 Ability to provide constructive criticism	1 ☐	2 ☐	3 ☐	4 ☐	5 ☐
11 Ability to accept constructive criticism	1 ☐	2 ☐	3 ☐	4 ☐	5 ☐
12 Ability to listen to others	1 ☐	2 ☐	3 ☐	4 ☐	5 ☐
13 Ability to persuade others to your point of view	1 ☐	2 ☐	3 ☐	4 ☐	5 ☐
14 Ability to plan ahead, setting realistic targets for departmental improvement	1 ☐	2 ☐	3 ☐	4 ☐	5 ☐
15 Ability to implement agreed plans	1 ☐	2 ☐	3 ☐	4 ☐	5 ☐
16 Ability to solve problems	1 ☐	2 ☐	3 ☐	4 ☐	5 ☐
17 Ability to use time effectively	1 ☐	2 ☐	3 ☐	4 ☐	5 ☐
18 Ability to manage stress	1 ☐	2 ☐	3 ☐	4 ☐	5 ☐
19 Ability to identify problems	1 ☐	2 ☐	3 ☐	4 ☐	5 ☐
20 Ability to understand whole school issues	1 ☐	2 ☐	3 ☐	4 ☐	5 ☐

Departmental development plan 199 /9

RB2

Organisation (broad outline)	Staff co-ordinator INSET implications Resource and financial implications Success criteria
Curriculum (target areas for development and planned stages of implementation)	Staff co-ordinator INSET implications Resource and financial implications Success criteria
Assessment	Staff co-ordinator INSET implications Resource and financial implications Success criteria
Whole-school priorities	Staff co-ordinator INSET implications Resource and financial implications Success criteria

Departmental development plan **RB3**

Priority

Targets

Resource implications
(including INSET)

Monitoring

Success criteria

Staff record sheet

RB4

Date ____________ Name ____________

Year ____________ Department ____________

Qualifications

Year appointed

Classes taught

Contact ratio

Exam syllabuses/ courses taught

Extra responsibilities

Extra curriculum activities

Appraisal process

INSET/courses attended

Other information

Personal staff development plan RB5

Name ______________________ Date ______________

Past year (courses, INSET, committees, curriculum development initiatives, departmental responsibilities, etc.)

Teaching/Tutorial commitment this year
(age, subject, levels, exam courses, etc.)

Interest/Experience in other subject areas or other levels

Future career development

Personal INSET/ development needs

Whole School/ Development needs

Action Plan

Signed ______________________ (Head of Department)

Signed ______________________ (Staff)

Departmental INSET planning form RB6

Departmental INSET ______________________________ 199__

Department ______________________________

Topic

Aims of the day

Programme:
(with details of timing for morning and afternoon sessions)

Provider in-house/visitor

Cost

Location/venue
(rooms and facilities required)

Signed ______________________________

INSET course evaluation form

RB7

Name ______________________________

Title of course ______________________________

Course providers ______________________________

Date ______________ Venue ______________

Funding for course:

Course aims:

How far did the course meet its aims and your INSET needs?

What action(s) if any are you going to take as a result of attending this course?

Would you recommend this course to other staff?

Stock list for books

RB8

No	Title	Author	Ability/level

Resources allocation form

RB9

Staff	Set	Term 1	Term 2	Term 3

Checklist for monitoring health and safety **RB10**

Do you know who the school's health and safety officer is?	Yes ☐ No ☐
Do you know of any specific health and safety matters relating to your department?	Yes ☐ No ☐
Is there a departmental policy for health and safety which is consistent with the overall school policy?	Yes ☐ No ☐
Are all members of your team aware of the health and safety policy?	Yes ☐ No ☐
Do members of your department team follow recommended health and safety procedures?	Yes ☐ No ☐
Do you regularly visually check all electrical items and report any suspected problems?	Yes ☐ No ☐
Do you know when was the last time electrical equipment was officially checked?	Yes ☐ No ☐
Do all teaching rooms have a clearly displayed fire notice?	Yes ☐ No ☐
Are fire exits clearly marked and do members of your department ensure that there is free access to them?	Yes ☐ No ☐
Do you know who is the nearest person in the school with medical/first aid training?	Yes ☐ No ☐
Have you got up-to-date lists of pupils' medical problems?	Yes ☐ No ☐
Are other staff in the department aware of these medical problems?	Yes ☐ No ☐
Do all members of the department know what to do in the event of an emergency?	Yes ☐ No ☐

Departmental planner

RB11

Month	To do: Details	Action	Completed

Departmental planner

RB12

Week no. & w/c	Department internal/ external coursework/ exams	Tutorial programme	School admin. meetings/parents' evenings	Visits, field trips, include work experience etc.	Sport and extra curricular activities	Assemblies

Personal planner

RB13

Subject	Action to be taken	Deadline	Follow-up

Daily planner

RB14

Date ______________________

Before school	**Notes**
Break	**Notes**
Lunch	**Notes**
After school	**Notes**

Administration tasks planner **RB15**

Task	Person responsible	Time-scale	Comments
Preparation of departmental handbook, including schemes of work			
Information to parents			
Allocation of existing pupils to classes, sets			
Examination preparation; i) internal ii) external iii) entries			
Pupil assessment, recording and reporting			
Pastoral care issues			
Careers guidance and pupil placement			
Staff induction			
Staff development programme			

Administration tasks planner RB15

Task	Person responsible	Time-scale	Comments
Requisition and ordering			
Stocktaking			
Budget and finances			
Health and safety			
Primary/tertiary liaison			
Special needs			
Departmental statistical information			
Parents' evenings			
Resources allocation			
Non-teaching staff			

Pupil referral form

RB16

Pupil name	Reason for referral	Source of referral	Action	Date

High School department liaison record

RB17

Name of department

Date

Member of staff

Feeder school

Staff contacted

Reason for contact

Outcome of contact

Name of department

Date

Member of staff

Feeder school

Staff contacted

Reason for contact

Outcome of contact

Name of department

Date

Member of staff

Feeder school

Staff contacted

Reason for contact

Outcome of contact

Name of department

Date

Member of staff

Feeder school

Staff contacted

Reason for contact

Outcome of contact

Key Stage 3 continuity and progression agreements

RB18

Curriculum	Resources	Assessment, recording and continuity	Targets for development
Year 7			
Year 8			
Year 9			

Time allocation Yr 7 Yr 8 Yr 9	**Liaison arrangements**
Feeder school 1	
Feeder school 2	

Checklist for good liaison with other establishments

RB19

Have all feeder schools got copies of the department's schemes of work?	Yes ☐ No ☐
Has the department got copies of the feeder school's schemes of work?	Yes ☐ No ☐
Do all members of the department team know who are the relevant staff to contact in each feeder school?	Yes ☐ No ☐
Do all members of the department team know about post-16 educational options?	Yes ☐ No ☐
Is there an agreement with all feeder schools about the nature of assessment before transfer?	Yes ☐ No ☐
Is there agreement about the nature of subject-specific records, and evidence of achievement and how these will be passed on from feeder schools?	Yes ☐ No ☐
Have any members of the department visited feeder schools or post-16 institutions this term?	Yes ☐ No ☐
Have staff from feeder schools and/or post-16 institutions been invited to any department meeting or activity this term?	Yes ☐ No ☐
Are there plans for any joint curriculum development with feeder schools or post-16 institutions?	Yes ☐ No ☐

Checklist for writing a department handbook

RB20

Do I have an up-to-date copy of the school's aims?		Yes ☐	No ☐
Do I have copies of exam board syllabuses?		Yes ☐	No ☐
Has the department got up-to-date aims and objectives?		Yes ☐	No ☐
Have I got copies of any departmental policies?		Yes ☐	No ☐
Are there detailed schemes of work for all courses taught in the department?		Yes ☐	No ☐
Has the department got a development plan?		Yes ☐	No ☐
Have I got details about the resources available?		Yes ☐	No ☐
Have I got details of:	staff qualifications?	Yes ☐	No ☐
	recent INSET?	Yes ☐	No ☐
	job descriptions?	Yes ☐	No ☐
	areas of responsibility?	Yes ☐	No ☐
	teaching commitment?	Yes ☐	No ☐
Have I got details of:	non-teaching staff hours?	Yes ☐	No ☐
	job descriptions?	Yes ☐	No ☐
	qualifications?	Yes ☐	No ☐
	recent INSET?	Yes ☐	No ☐
Do I have information about health and safety procedures in the department?		Yes ☐	No ☐

Planning grid for scheme of work **RB21**

Topic: **Stage:** **Year:**

Key questions	Concepts/terminology	Teaching & learning	Resources	Homework

Planning grid for scheme of work RB22

Topic:			**Lesson:**		
Content	Resources	Core	Extension work for most able	Approach for less able	Homework

Planning grid for scheme of work RB23

	Content	Resource	Task	Pupil outcome	Teacher response
Level 1–3					
Level 3–6					
Level 6–10					

Checklist for choosing a syllabus **RB24**

Is there a good match between the expertise of the department and the demands of the syllabus?	Yes ☐	No ☐
Are the exam results with this syllabus satisfactory?	Yes ☐	No ☐
Is the balance between coursework and final assessment satisfactory?	Yes ☐	No ☐
Are other syllabuses available?	Yes ☐	No ☐
Do members of the department have experience of teaching other syllabuses?	Yes ☐	No ☐
Have students expressed any preferences about the syllabus?	Yes ☐	No ☐
Would there be any resource implications in changing the syllabus?	Yes ☐	No ☐

Curriculum development proposal

RB25

Subject

Head of Department

What is the title of the proposed course?	
Which exam board/organising body?	
Contact name/tel. no. for further information.	
What age range of pupils is the course intended for?	
What is the proposed start date for the course?	
What is the duration of the proposed course?	
Which (if any) course will be replaced by this course?	
What are the minimum and maximum pupil numbers for the viability of this proposal?	
What are the costs per pupil of exam entry?	
How many teaching periods will this proposal require?	
What will be the cost of this teaching commitment? (using an average cost of ____ per teaching period)	
Give names of existing staff who are qualified to teach this course.	
Will additional staff be needed to teach this course?	
What will be the implications for the rest of the courses taught by the department if this proposal is adopted?	

Signed ______________________ Date ______________________

Please give copies of this proposal to: ______________________

Curriculum development proposal

RB25

Subject

Head of Department

Will staff need INSET or have to attend exam board meetings? Give details including number of days and costs of supply cover and teacher travel per year.	
Will the proposal require the use of additional or specialist rooms? Give details.	
Will clerical/technician support be required? Give details including proposed hours and estimated costs per year.	
Will the proposal require teaching/learning materials? If so, what will be the overall costs? (Please attach detailed list with costs.)	
What will be the maintenance costs of the proposal? (i.e. stationery, replacement of texts, etc.)	
Will the proposal require additional equipment? Give details including costs.	
Will the proposal require the use of additional school facilities e.g. the use of the school hall in the evening for a performance? Give details including costs of additional caretaker hours.	
What are the total costs of any visits or field trips? Attach detailed lists (e.g. travel, financial support for pupils on low incomes, etc.) What are the proposed dates?	
Does the proposal include assessment arrangements which may involve the use of supply cover e.g. orals, aurals? Give details including proposed dates, supply teacher hours required and their cost.	
What are the approximate total costs of this proposal?	
Give reasons for proposing this curriculum development.	

Signed ______________________ Date ______________________

Please give copies of this proposal to: ______________________

Curriculum development proposal

RB26

Subject

Name(s) of staff involved ______________________________

Nature of proposed development

Age range

Examination Board/organising body

Date of proposed start

Staffing implications of proposed development
e.g. number of teaching periods required, staff who are qualified to teach proposed course, additional staffing required etc.

Resource implications of proposed change
e.g. accommodation, equipment, INSET, exam entry costs, teaching/learning materials, supply cover needed.

Total anticipated costs £ ______________________________

Justification for this curriculum development proposal
How will proposal help school to meet its aims, how will it be better than existing provision?

Discussed/Approved

Action planning sheet

RB27

Issue from report

Objective

Action proposed

Responsible person and people involved

Time-scale

Resources allocated

Headings for evaluation report and indicators of improvement selected

Action planning sheet

RB28

Priority	Coordinator	Time-scale
First term (Target 1)	Second term (Target 2)	Third term (Target 3)
Tasks	Tasks	Tasks
Success criteria	Success criteria	Success criteria
Resources	Resources	Resources

Action planning sheet

RB29

Issue ______________________ Date ______________

Team involved ______________ Team leader ______________ Supported by ______________

Task	Resources (item/cost)	INSET needs	What has been achieved?

Start by	By whom	Finish by

Task	Resources (item/cost)	INSET needs	What has been achieved?

Start by	By whom	Finish by

Task	Resources (item/cost)	INSET needs	What has been achieved?

Start by	By whom	Finish by

Future targets

Action planning sheet

RB30

Priority

Action plan

Action steps

Support needs
Items ______ Cost ______
Items ______ Cost ______
Items ______ Cost ______

Evaluation

Specific outcomes

Gathering data

Priority

Action plan

Action steps

Support needs
Items ______ Cost ______
Items ______ Cost ______
Items ______ Cost ______

Evaluation

Specific outcomes

Gathering data

Priority

Action plan

Action steps

Support needs
Items ______ Cost ______
Items ______ Cost ______
Items ______ Cost ______

Evaluation

Specific outcomes

Gathering data